I0820755

Foreword by Priscilla Shirer

GOD IS

60 Days of Learning Who God Is to Understand Who We Are

For Teen Girls

Alena Franklin

Published by B&H Publishing Group, Brentwood, Tennessee

979-8-3845-1563-0
Dewey Decimal Classification: 248.3
Subject Heading: GIRLS / PRAYERS / DEVOTIONAL LITERATURE

Author uses italic for emphasis when quoting Scripture.

Manufactured in Shenzhen, Guangdong, China by Asia Pacific, April 2025
1 2 3 4 5 6 7 • 29 28 27 26 25

CONTENTS

FOREWORD

Priscilla Shirer

My phone buzzed and beeped simultaneously. I grabbed it from the kitchen counter and looked down at the notification banner—*"Alena."* My face melted into a warm smile at the sight of my niece's name, the same way it always does when she texts me. I swiped up in anticipation about what the message might say.

You never know with the two of us. Our text thread topics range from corny jokes we've overheard to workout regimens we want to try. We alert each other to new recipes we should cook and curly-girl hairstyles we think the other should explore. We send links for the latest fashion trends we should wear and for musical artists and songs we need to add to our ever-growing playlists.

"Auntie Silla, download 'I Think He Is' by Rita Springer asap."

I did. And I've had this song on constant rotation ever since.

The song itself is an anthem really—a declaration about the unchanging character of God that holds steady even when life doesn't. *Especially* when it doesn't. Each stanza paints a picture of hard moments—the mountains, deserts, and valleys—and the staying power of a loving and good Father who brings us through them all. The jewel of the lyrics is found in a chorus that asks, *"Is God still good?"* and then immediately responds, *"Oh, I think He is."* Then, slowly but surely, the melody builds in intensity and assurance to the very end, where the question it asks is the same, but the reply is different.

"Is God still good? Oh, I KNOW He is."

Alena's confidence in God's character is something she's unearthed over time, during the kind of hardships this songwriter describes. Her young life has been marked by its fair share of heartache, as well as by the beauty of many joys and triumphs. The ebbs and flows have taken her on a roller-coaster ride of self-discovery and sacred calling. Even in her youth, Alena has had to come to grips with a reality many believers don't settle into until their hair turns gray: Do we merely *think* God is good and faithful and worth serving, or do we truly *know* it in the depths of our souls? Because *knowing* is everything.

Knowing His character is unchanging.

Knowing His goodness is unflappable.

Knowing who GOD IS.

And I can't think of any young woman who is more equipped and divinely suited to share these truths with you than Alena Franklin.

I admit without reservation that I'm partial to her. She is, after all, one of my best friends and part of my family. But my reasons run far deeper than that. Alena's voice is raw and authentic, unspoiled by the need to impress people. She's been through too much. She's needed God too desperately to write a book filled with untested platitudes and hollow sentiments. Instead, she writes with a wisdom, integrity, and humility that makes you want to trust the Father as much as she does. These pages will inspire you to drill your roots down deeply into the soil of God's character so that you'll be anchored in every season of your life.

Little sister, the Lord has led you to this book, and the timing of it reaching you is not happenstance. Every detail of your life—the easy and the difficult, the convenient and the uncomfortable, the joyful and the downright unbearable—has softened the soil of your heart to absorb these insights with a tenderness and receptiveness you might not otherwise have. You are about to be introduced to your Father again with the fresh vision that your circumstances have cultivated. Or maybe this will be your very first time coming face-to-face with the One who will never disappoint you like so many others have. Either way, pour yourself a latte, pull up a chair to the conversation, ask the Lord to reveal Himself to you, and then turn the page.

Are you wondering if He is really able to carry you through life's hardships and hurts?

Are you questioning if He is worth serving when doing so feels isolating and sticky?

Have you wondered if He is a suitable Savior, able to rescue you from a mess you may have created with your own rebellion or indifference?

Are you questioning whether or not He is patient enough, long-suffering enough, merciful enough, powerful enough to control the chaos you may see swirling around you?

Lean in and listen to your Auntie Silla, little sister . . .

I know He is.

INTRODUCTION

Hey, you.

If you're holding this book right now, I believe it's for you.

(Seriously, I prayed you would be here.)

Whether you picked this book up on your own or a loved one forced it into your hands, I'm really glad you showed up. I encourage you to KEEP reading!

When my life got turned upside down going into my freshman year of high school, so did my view of God. A month before ninth grade, my mom died. A month after that, we moved to a brand-new city. Everything I'd ever known felt shaky and untrustworthy. I found myself with more questions than answers.

Why did God allow my mom to die?

Why don't I feel like I belong?

Can I actually trust God?

Does God even like me?

What I knew about God at that time in my life proved not to be enough, and I began searching for who God *really* was—who He really *is*. I knew God fit in the grand scheme of life, but I had to figure out how God fit into the intricacies of my own story . . . and where I fit into His story.

That journey led me here.

This devotional is the remnants of my wrestling with God the past six years. Written in these pages are truths the Bible points us to about who God is in the highs, lows, and in-betweens of our lives. The great thing is that God will never change. He is the same yesterday, today, and tomorrow.

When I lifted my eyes to see God in the middle of my suffering, I found the answers I had been searching for. I knew I belonged to God, and I knew I could trust Him. Not only does He like me—He loves me.

It's impossible to capture all of who God is in sixty devotions, but I pray these words serve as a foundation for whom you believe Him to be for the REST of your life.

The Bible promises that when we seek God, we will find Him (Jeremiah 29:13). If you're still reading, congratulations—you're seeking!

As you search, I pray that you find what you're looking for. May these words help you find the faith to trust God, for the first time or again. May they help you understand who you are. And may you come to know God as the One who has been for you from the very beginning.

The more you know God, the more you'll understand yourself. I know it. Why? Because I am His child. I look to who He is to better understand who I am. And so can you.

So who is God? Let's find out together.

None Like Him

For this is what the high and exalted One says—
he who lives forever, whose name is holy:
"I live in a high and holy place,
but also with the one who is contrite and lowly of spirit,
to revive the spirit of the lowly
and to revive the heart of the contrite."

—Isaiah 57:15

GOD IS PERFECT

He is the Rock, his works are perfect, and all his ways are just. A faithful God who does no wrong, upright and just is he.
—DEUTERONOMY 32:4

God is perfect. He is completely whole, right, and just, *always*.

It's hard to wrap our minds around the perfection of God. Maybe it's because perfection is something most of us are continually striving for and always falling short of. As a natural performer and achiever, striving for perfection is like a game to me—a game I've been losing my entire life. Whether it's writing the perfect sentence or recording a flawless video, very rarely am I fully satisfied with my creation. And even when I am satisfied, I am sure my work *still* isn't perfect.

If I can't do normal tasks perfectly, how much greater must my imperfection be before God? The unspeakable thoughts that bounce around in my mind, the way I speak to my sister or the gossip I take part in with my friends—these kinds of things only scratch the surface of my sin. If I serve a perfect God, how can He possibly love someone as imperfect as me?

Yet He loves me. You too. God loves us so much that He paid the price to overcome our sin—the cost of *our* imperfection.

Jesus, the Son of God, came to earth, lived a perfect, sin-free life, and then paid the price for our imperfection on the cross. His sinlessness makes up for our lack, and because of His love, He covers us with His perfection. Don't get me wrong. After we accept Jesus's perfection, we will still sin. You have probably sinned today. I know I have. Maybe you said or did something you wish you could take back. Maybe you replay the events by thinking, *If only I...* or, *If I just could...*

God is deeply aware of our shortcomings and our brokenness. He calls us to pursue what is right, but He knows we can't obtain perfection *on our own*. It's not possible. He calls us to accept Jesus's perfect sacrifice for our sins, to make Him the King of our lives, and to live lives that honor Him. Then, He sends us His Holy Spirit, who is slowly making us more like God's Son, Jesus.

God lacks flaws. Something about this is such a relief. The God of the universe has got it all together. *Phew*. Rather than making an idol out of perfection and trying to get it all right, try leaning into the righteousness and perfection of God the Son. He paid the cost so we wouldn't have to. One day, God will make all His people perfect again. Until then, we don't have to be afraid that our imperfections will make us guilty before God.

We have a perfect God. He is more righteous and just than we can ever know. He knows our imperfections, and He still chooses us. Our flaws don't scare Him. Let God's righteousness wash over you, *helping* you embrace Jesus's perfection. Rather than lingering on what you could have done better, thank God that His Son did it best. Rest in Jesus's perfection.

FURTHER READING: 2 CORINTHIANS 12:9

- *Is perfectionism something you struggle with? How?*
- *If you are in Christ, His perfection extends to you. How does that change your life?*
- *How does it feel to know that God is perfect?*

BECAUSE GOD IS PERFECT, I CAN TRUST THAT JESUS HAS COVERED ALL MY SIN.

GOD IS THREE IN ONE

"Therefore go and make disciples of all nations, baptizing them in the name of the Father and of the Son and of the Holy Spirit."

—MATTHEW 28:19 CSB

God is three in one.

God is Father.

God is Son, Jesus Christ.

God is Holy Spirit.

God doesn't stop being one to be another. He is all three at the same time: our Father, our Savior, and our Advocate. The church calls this the Trinity.

Have you ever noticed how many people we need daily? It didn't take me long to realize that God places different people in our lives for different things. Practically speaking, we don't call our science teacher to help us with English homework. Our parents don't call the pool guy to take care of electrical problems. You and I don't call our friend who's in a hard spot to lightheartedly chat about how fun life is.

The Bible makes it clear that God plays many roles. He *has* many roles. And the beauty of God is that He is not limited. His divinity allows Him to be and to do more than we ever could. God the Father created us. God the Son came to earth and saved us. And God the Holy Spirit guides and sustains us. The Father, Son, and Holy Spirit are distinct persons, with different roles. The difference between my example and the Trinity is that the Father, Son, and Spirit are all *one* God. The Father is not the Son, the Son is not the Spirit, and the Spirit is not the Father. Jesus is God, but He is not the Father or the Spirit. The Holy Spirit is God, but He is not the Son or the Father.

God's three-in-oneness may feel confusing. Remember, as humans, we are limited in our understanding and abilities. Our minds can't comprehend too much at once, let alone fully understand how God is three in one. The God who made you can hold and handle any problem you face and any question you have. Ask Him to help you understand the Trinity as best you can.

After all, God's three-in-oneness (or triunity) makes Him distinct. Our God is unlike any god of any other religion and better than what anyone can conjure up or imagine. Since the beginning of time, God has been living in love for all of eternity.

Being the Trinity is who God is.

Further Reading: Genesis 1:26

- *Have you heard of God being three in one (triune) before? When?*
- *What changes about your view of God when you believe He is three in one?*
- *What are some questions you have about God being the Trinity?*

BECAUSE GOD IS A TRINITY,
I BELIEVE HE IS UNLIKE ANY OTHER
IDEA OF GOD THAT EXISTS.

God Is Righteous

"Declare what is to be, present it—let them take counsel together. Who foretold this long ago, who declared it from the distant past? Was it not I, the Lord*? And there is no God apart from me, a righteous God and a Savior; there is none but me."*

—Isaiah 45:21

God is righteous. He is morally right and just all the time—no exceptions.

Have you ever had a friend or acquaintance who thought they were always right? Their pride sucked up the air around them, and very few people wanted to be their friend. Because they thought they were always right, they walked around judging everyone else for what they didn't do perfectly. That is called *self-righteousness*—when someone sees their morality as perfect and their actions as just. Maybe you've been there yourself. I know I have. (Be careful, it's an easy bug to catch.)

This isn't who God is. He is not *self*-righteous. He is *righteousness Himself*.

Morality and justice overflow from God's character. Moral codes, justice, and goodness wouldn't exist without Him.

God is the standard for righteousness, and righteousness is unattainable outside of Him.

God isn't like the self-righteousness we tend to have. He is always right and always just and has every right to flaunt every bit of it. God's righteousness also is humble and meek. (We see this throughout Jesus's life.) When God points out His righteousness and glory, it's not a brag—it's a fact. It's not prideful. It is weighty though. We know what is right *because* of Him.

The best part is that God doesn't keep His righteousness to Himself. He doesn't withhold it or wave His finger in our faces when we fall short of it. Instead, He extended His righteousness to us by sending His only Son to die for us so we could be clothed in His righteousness too. Second Corinthians 5:21 says, "God made him who had no sin to be sin for us, so that in him we might become the righteousness of God."

When we accept Jesus's sacrifice as payment for our sins, God sees us as though we are covered in Jesus's sinlessness. On our own, we are unrighteous, constantly wrong, and like chickens with our heads cut off, running around trying to prove we are good enough for God! With God, however, we are called righteous. Not because we are, but because *He is*.

FURTHER READING: EPHESIANS 4:24

- *In your own words, what does it mean to be righteous?*
- *If God is the only truly righteous One, what does that mean for us?*
- *Do you live like you're clothed in God's righteousness? Why or why not?*

BECAUSE GOD IS RIGHTEOUS,
I DON'T HAVE TO TRY TO EARN
GOD'S LOVE ON MY OWN.

GOD IS TRUTH

Jesus answered, "I am the way and the truth and the life. No one comes to the Father except through me."
—JOHN 14:6

God is Truth. He is the right answer, the only way, and without error.

Truth has been a controversial concept since . . . well, all of time. Since almost the beginning, humans have tried to create their own rules to replace the ones they didn't like. It started when Satan asked Adam and Eve if God *really* said they would die if they ate the fruit in Genesis 3, and it has continued ever since.

The stories around truth are confusing because we can never quite land on what's true on our own. Laws are altered, and textbooks are changed. It's common to use the phrase, "my truth." It's hard growing up today! We're all a little confused. If I have a truth and you have a different truth, how can anything be true?

God clears up all our questions and concerns in John 14:6. Jesus tells us that He *is* truth, and no one can come to God except through Him.

If Jesus is Truth, Jesus is God, and God inspired the Bible, then the easiest way we can find God's truth is by reading God's Word. God's Word is truth in written form. God informs us that all Scripture is God-breathed and trustworthy (2 Timothy 3:16–17). We can take our big questions and concerns to it because it has the answers.

God's Word was written down thousands of years ago by followers of God inspired by the Holy Spirit *to* real Christians living in real places and times. It is also *alive*. Hebrews 4:12 tells us that God's Word is living and active, "sharper than any double-edged sword." The Holy Spirit who helped people write down the words of the Bible is the same Spirit helping you understand as you read today. His truth will always pierce through lies.

Satan knows the quickest way to our hearts is to get us to believe lies. He's been doing it since Genesis 3, when Adam and Eve believed God was lying to them, and it's why Jesus calls him the "father of lies" (John 8:44). But we don't have to believe him; we actually have the power to resist Satan's lies and live in the truth that God speaks over us. How? By getting really familiar with the voice of Jesus. Jesus said, "I am the good shepherd. . . . My sheep hear my voice, I know them, and they follow me" (John 10:11, 27).

The best way to know the truth of God from the lies of the devil is to listen to the voice of Jesus by reading His Word, meditating on it, and remembering it.

As Satan's voice and the world around us get noisier, don't forget that God is truth. When we read God's Word and spend time with Him, we remember the truth when the enemy attacks us with lies.

Everything God says is true because He is Truth. Press into His Word and fight for truth.

Further Reading: Hebrews 4:12

- *Look up the definition of* truth *and write it down.*
- *If God is truth, what does that mean for your life?*
- *What are you fighting to believe is true in God's Word?*

BECAUSE GOD IS TRUTH, I DON'T HAVE TO WONDER WHAT IS TRUE.

GOD IS HOLY

Each of the four living creatures had six wings and was covered with eyes all around, even under its wings. Day and night they never stop saying: "'Holy, holy, holy is the LORD GOD *Almighty,' who was, and is, and is to come."*

—REVELATION 4:8

God is holy. He is set apart from everyone and everything. There is no one like Him.

I grew up hearing about God's holiness. I sang songs and listened to prayers about how holy God is. But to be completely honest, I had no idea what God's holiness *meant*. Was it about God's rules? Was it about how much better one person was than another? As I got older, the word became stale and dormant to me (ironic, because that is the total opposite of what holiness is).

Holiness is defined as "set apart" or "sacred." God is the Creator of *all* things; everything is created by Him. Because He alone is the Creator, He is completely different from everything else—utterly set apart. He is perfect in purity, righteousness, and goodness. His perfection makes Him holy. Holiness is the last word our minds should grow numb to.

If the reality of God's holiness overwhelms you, it should. But it should also comfort you. He is holy, and He is *our* God.

God's perfection and "set apartness" are nothing like anything we know. The God of the universe is better than all of us in every sense.

So how do we respond? We praise Him. Because God is holy, He is worthy of our worship. We live in awe of Him, overwhelmed and incredibly thankful because, unlike what you might think, God has made it so that His holiness doesn't separate us from being with Him. On our own, our lack of holiness keeps us from being able to spend eternity with God. But when Jesus died in our place, He made a way for us to be set apart like He is—to become beloved children of a holy God. Our sins are covered by His perfection, and we can be set apart too.

God is holy, and we still get to be with Him. God is perfect, yet He still wants to hear from and *be* with us. There is nothing stale or dormant about that!

Overwhelm. Awe. Comfort. We can experience all these things because the God who made us is perfect and set apart. We can trust Him because He is holy.

FURTHER READING: ISAIAH 6:3

- *Have you ever thought about the holiness of God? Do you think about it any differently today?*
- *What does God's holiness mean to you?*
- *How does it feel to have a perfect God who still wants to be with you?*

BECAUSE GOD IS HOLY, I CAN TRUST THAT HE IS BETTER THAN ANYONE OR ANYTHING ELSE.

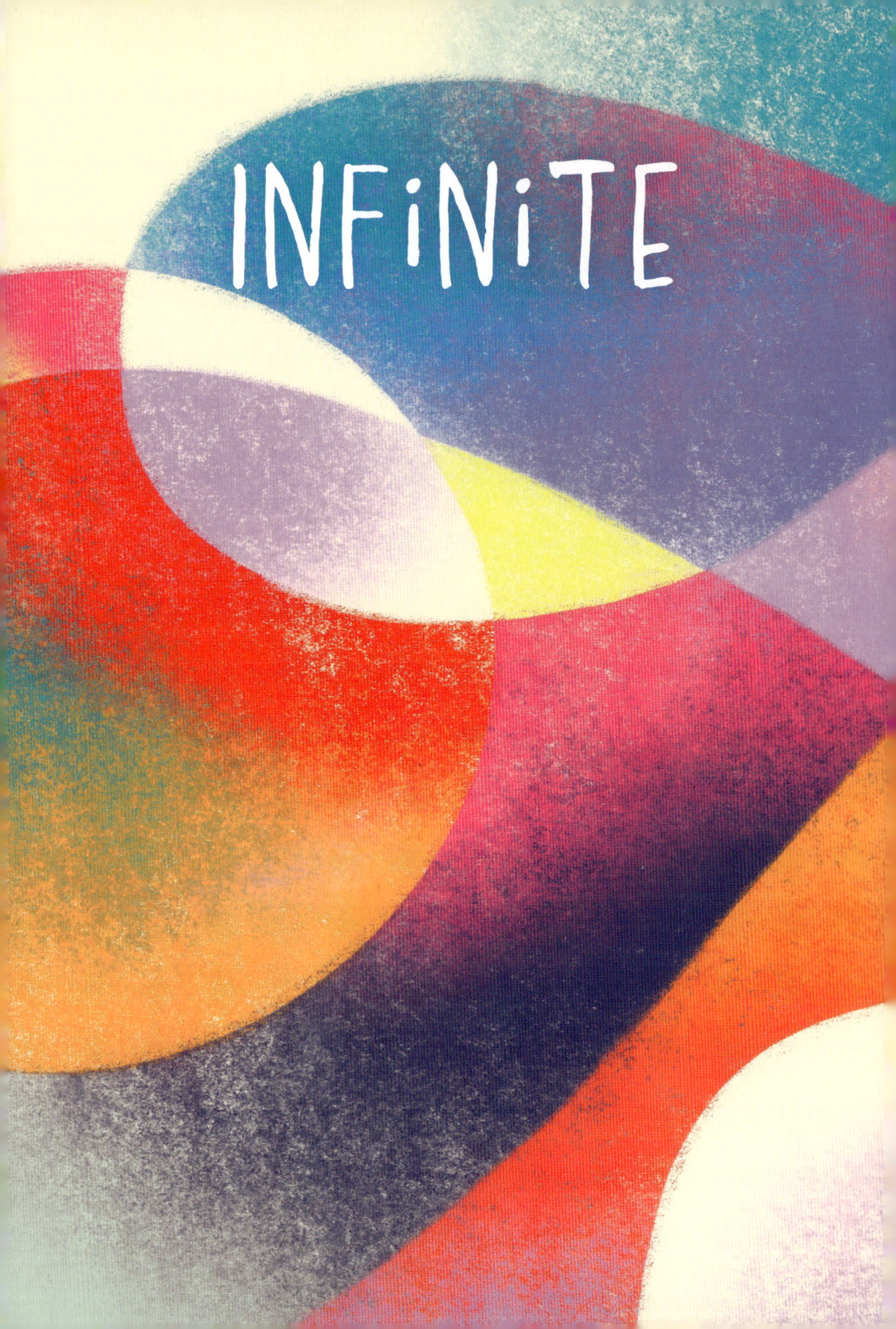
INFINITE

Before the mountains were born
or you brought forth the whole world,
from everlasting to everlasting you are God.
—Psalm 90:2

GOD IS SELF-EXISTENT

God said to Moses, "I AM WHO I AM. This is what you are to say to the Israelites: 'I AM has sent me to you.'"

—EXODUS 3:14

The Bible is filled with jaw-dropping one-liners from God. My favorite is found in Exodus, when Moses stumbled across a burning bush.

The Bible tells us that Moses was tending to his father-in-law's flock when he saw a bush on fire but not burning up. Moses went to it, curious why the bush had not shriveled up. God then called to him from the bush! He told Moses that He was going to send him to Pharoah and demand that the Israelites be set free from captivity in Egypt. Like any human, Moses responded to this great call with fear and a sense of inferiority. In Exodus 3:14, Moses asked God what he should tell the Israelites about who sent him. God responded, " I AM WHO I AM."

What a riddle! If I were Moses, I might have scratched my head a bit in sheer confusion. What was God telling Moses about Himself? That He is self-existent. You and I need water, air, and food to stay alive. We need love, care, and affection to thrive. God needs none of this. He existed before water. His presence was here before planet Earth itself. He doesn't have a mother who brought Him into existence and nurtured Him. He has always been and will always be *God*.

If that thought overwhelms you, you are not alone. It's hard to wrap our minds around the existence of One who has no beginning. You and I were *created*, and we will eventually die. No matter how hard we study, we can't know everything! God, however, cannot die because He was not created. He knows everything and doesn't even study! He depends on nothing and no one to exist.

The essence of God, His self-existing nature, can feel like a made-up story from a movie. Sometimes God can feel far off or even scary. But the truth is, God existing on His own should offer us great comfort and stability. The Author of our stories and Creator of our bodies doesn't need *anything* from us or anyone else. This means He can love us freely without needing anything in return. He isn't dependent on us, and therefore, we are not crushed by His expectations.

In ancient Egyptian culture, pharaohs were considered gods. But of course, they were born, they died, and each one was replaced by the next pharaoh. God was telling Pharoah, Moses, and anyone who would listen to this great truth: God has been, and He will always be, and He doesn't need anyone to help with that. He is greater than "god," and His desire is for the good of His people. If we are His, we will always be taken care of.

God's nature can be hard to grasp, but He is not some far-off idea or dream. He will always exist, and we get to spend our lives getting to know Him.

Further Reading: John 1:1–5

- *What characteristic of God most surprises you?*
- *How can you get more curious about who God is?*
- *Does God's nature comfort you or scare you? What would help change that?*

BECAUSE GOD IS SELF-EXISTENT,
I BELIEVE HE IS ALL I NEED.

GOD IS ETERNAL

Now to the King eternal, immortal, invisible, the only God, be honor and glory for ever and ever. Amen.

—1 TIMOTHY 1:17

God is eternal. He has no beginning or end. He exists fully outside of time. In the previous devotion, we unpacked God's self-existence. Part of that truth is that there hasn't been a day when He didn't exist, and there won't ever be a day when He doesn't exist. If you think about it too hard, you might feel like your head will explode.

I have struggled with this concept my entire life. How could someone exist *forever*, completely unbound by time as we know it?

For years, I would wake up and be tormented by the thought of existing eternally. I'd think about the question that used to stump my faith: *If God created everything, who created God?* I'd spiral and spiral until my mind exhausted itself.

In retrospect, I realize Satan was just trying to dampen the awe and wonder I should hold at the mystery of God. That is what God's eternality is after all. A *mystery*.

As humans, we only know beginnings and endings. God created us to live in time. Our lives reflect that sequence. We are born, and we die. We start, and we end. We are mortals, so it's no surprise that God's eternal nature would seem foreign to us!

Luckily, our minds don't have to fully comprehend what eternity means for it to be true. We may exist inside of time, but God doesn't.

Do you want to know something amazing? God created us with a version of this eternality.

Unlike God, we have a clear beginning, but although our bodies will die, our souls will live on forever. God loves us so much that He made a way for us to spend forever *with* Him. When we accept His grace, we're promised that we'll live forever with Him—our bodies *and* our souls.

The fact that God is eternal doesn't need to be something we fully comprehend now. God's eternal nature makes Him the most reliable being ever to exist. If anyone knows the ins and outs of life, it's Him. Because He is outside of time, God knows it all, and He is with you in the middle of everything. God is eternal in His existence, His love, and His truth. His love for you has no beginning or end, His truth won't ever expire, and He has never not been God. Rest in that.

Further Reading: Psalm 90:1–2

- *What does it mean for God to be eternal?*
- *How does God's eternality make you feel?*
- *What is good about God existing forever?*

BECAUSE GOD IS ETERNAL, I AM INVITED TO LIVE WITH HIM FOREVER.

GOD IS BETTER

The LORD is exalted over all the nations, his glory above the heavens. Who is like the LORD our God, the One who sits enthroned on high, who stoops down to look on the heavens and the earth?

—PSALM 113:4–6

God is infinitely better than anything else. There is no one like Him, not even a little bit.

It's hard to believe that Someone you can't physically see could be better than all the amazing things you *can* see. But it's true.

It's like looking at pictures of a beautiful place. Bora Bora, for example. It's a stunning destination. If you typed it in Google, you'd see stunning photos. The water is crystal blue, and the reviews talk a big game, but it's not until you go that you realize how magnificent Bora Bora is—way better than the photos!

And God is better than that.

God's love is better than a boy's affection. You won't find unconditional love anywhere else. God's Word is better than your favorite book. Every ounce of it is true because God cannot lie. God's heart is better than your most caring friend. His motives are only good, and He loves all things that are rooted in love, joy, peace, patience, kindness, faithfulness, goodness, gentleness, and self-control.

Yes, He gives us good gifts, including people to love, books to read, friends to trust, and more. He has gifted each of us uniquely, with talents and dreams. He has blessed us with beauty all around, giving us a breathtaking world to live in. And He has kindly given us the grace to be like Him, despite our very human flaws. But do you believe that God, the greatest gift giver, is better than all the things He can give us?

It's hard to believe God is better than the enticing things around us. It's not easy to trust that what He has in mind is better than what we want for ourselves. You may ask Him for something good, and His answer may be *no*. Do you still trust Him? The reward of trusting is worth it. When you choose to believe that God is better, you'll always be satisfied because you always have Him. He is where true joy is found.

God wants you to choose Him. He wants you to trust Him with the gifts and blessings He has given you. And He wants you to believe that the Giver is *always* better than the gift.

Further Reading: James 1:17

- *What is the hardest thing about believing that God is better?*
- *What do you tend to believe is better than God?*
- *If you believed that God is better than everything else, how would your life change?*

BECAUSE GOD IS BETTER THAN ANYTHING, IF I HAVE HIM, I HAVE EVERYTHING.

GOD IS ALIVE

The LORD lives! Praise be to my Rock!
Exalted be God my Savior!
—PSALM 18:46

God is alive! He is more alive than anything we see here on earth—God is living and breathing all around us. His Spirit is alive in His creation, in heaven, and everywhere in between. His Son is alive and is seated with God the Father. Our three-in-one God rules and reigns over the whole earth.

It's hard to believe in someone you cannot lay eyes on. It's hard to understand how someone you've *never* seen could be more alive than anything you've *ever* seen. But did you know you can see God's aliveness in all His creation?

Roman 1:20 tells us that God's invisible qualities can be seen through what He has made. So when we look at the world He created—trees swaying as the wind blows, birds chirping, and the sun shining or thunder rolling—we are reminded of God's presence in real time. All of this came from God.

God's goodness in creation displays His aliveness.

He has been moving and working since the beginning of time, and He never stopped.

This world will try to convince you that faith in God is dead. Useless. Not even real. But I'm here to tell you that the Spirit of God is more alive, useful, and more real than anything you've ever experienced.

God *is* life.

His Spirit has the power to give life and revive life. Jesus rose from the grave to give us life. We live only because of Him.

God's living power is active, and He wants to be active in your life too. Maybe doubts creep into your mind and you struggle to believe He's real. Maybe you love God with your entire heart and you know that He lives. No matter where you are in your walk with God, He loves you. He is the Giver of life and life everlasting, and you can ask Him to remind you that He is more real—more alive—than anything or anyone else.

God's light does not dim. He is not like an old lamp flickering out. He is brighter than the sun, and He shines all around you. Look at creation and remember that He is alive and with you. His presence is revealed before your eyes.

Further Reading: Romans 1:20

- *Do you believe that God is alive? When was the first time you believed this?*
- *In your own words, write down what it means that God is alive.*
- *What does it feel like to know that God is still moving and working today?*

BECAUSE GOD IS ALIVE,
I CAN HAVE LIFE TOO.

GOD IS OUR MAKER

I praise you because I am fearfully and wonderfully made; your works are wonderful, I know that full well. My frame was not hidden from you when I was made in the secret place, when I was woven together in the depths of the earth. Your eyes saw my unformed body; all the days ordained for me were written in your book before one of them came to be.

—PSALM 139:14–16

Our God is an infinitely thoughtful and intentional artist, and when He meticulously pieced you together, He called you *wonderful*.

Not long ago, I was trying on swimsuits, only to rip them off in hatred toward my body. Only two months until my wedding, I became unusually aware of every single detail of my frame. From the feeling of my thighs touching to how my arms looked when I relaxed, I picked myself apart until there was nothing left to pick.

Maybe you've felt the same way. You may not be preparing for a wedding, but perhaps you have become aware of the tiniest details of your body. You might hate the way your voice sounds when you hear yourself on video. Maybe you can't stand the way your stomach folds over when you sit. Perhaps you have a disability that limits what you can and can't do. You may even wonder if God *intentionally* created you this way.

He undoubtedly formed you with much more in mind than just your physical appearance, although He did make that a special part of who you are. He sees every part of you as His beautiful creation. He longs for you to see the same. And God can use you, no matter your physical state, to glorify Him. One day, every part of you that has been affected by this broken world will be made new and complete.

As I sulked on my bedroom floor, surrounded by a pile of too-small swimsuits, God kindly reminded me that I was thoughtfully designed. How could I hate something He knitted together with intentionality and beauty? I asked Him to show me what He sees. You can do the same.

You were fearfully and wonderfully created by the most wonderful, skilled artist. Because He is wonderful, what He makes is wonderful. He knows you better than you know yourself, and when He created you, He was pleased.

FURTHER READING: ISAIAH 45:12

- *What parts of yourself make it hard to believe that God created you on purpose?*
- *How does Psalm 139 change your view of God's unique design for you?*
- *How will you intentionally grow in love for every part of yourself?*

BECAUSE I HAVE A WONDERFUL MAKER, I CAN TRUST THAT HE INTENTIONALLY MADE EACH PART OF ME.

OMNIPOTENT

The Son is the radiance of God's glory and the exact representation of his being, sustaining all things by his powerful word. After he had provided purification for sins, he sat down at the right hand of the Majesty in heaven.

—HEBREWS 1:3

God Is Sovereign

He is before all things, and in him all things hold together.

—Colossians 1:17

God is the Creator and Sustainer of everything. Before anything was made, He existed. And because of this, God has control of it all. He is *sovereign*.

What are you in charge of? Perhaps you're the leader of a club at school or in charge of a particular chore at home. Growing up, my three sisters and I each had a separate domain in the house we were responsible for cleaning. (My dad used to be in the military, so he ran a tight ship, and he is passionate about responsibility and ownership. Hence why my sisters and I had "domains.") My domain was the kitchen, and it was my job to keep it spotless.

Each Saturday, I took care of that kitchen. I did my best to keep it in good condition so I didn't have to redo everything when my dad came to check. If my sisters came downstairs and started making a mess, I'd get upset. How could they ruin my work before my dad could even see it?

God has a domain. It just happens to be a lot more significant than my little kitchen.

Psalm 24 tells us that the earth and everything in it belong to God. And Colossians tells us that He holds *all things* together—more than just the earth! He is the landlord over it all, and He's not just any old landlord. No. God cares deeply for everything He makes. He cares about you and me, the flowers and grass, the animals and birds, and everything else in His creation.

Like any good leader, God takes good care of His children and creation. We don't have to question His power and ability or worry whether He knows what He is doing. God is the supreme Ruler, the highest in rank. He knows us better than we know ourselves, and He knows the earth better than even the greatest of scientists. God is in control.

God's ultimate sovereignty, coupled with our free will, can make for some beautiful things here on earth. But our free will can also make for some really bad things. He allowed us to bring sin into the world, and He allows sin to exist in the world today. However, because God is in control, we can't mess up His plan, even in our greatest sin. He is in control, and we can choose to join in His plan.

God doesn't need us for His will to reign. He doesn't need anything. He is the One who breathed life into us, and He is the Author of our days. He holds it all together. When you find yourself grasping for control of your tiny domain, remember that you don't have it. God does, and trust me, it's a lot better that way.

Further Reading: Psalm 24:1

- *Do you believe that God is sovereign? Why or why not?*
- *Where have you seen God's sovereignty in your life?*
- *How should the truth that God is sovereign affect how you live?*

BECAUSE GOD IS SOVEREIGN, I CAN LET GO OF MY NEED FOR CONTROL.

GOD IS MAJESTIC

"Who among the gods is like you, LORD?
Who is like you—majestic in holiness,
awesome in glory, working wonders?"
—EXODUS 15:11

Have you ever seen something so wondrous that your mind couldn't comprehend it?

Perhaps it was a sunset with beauty so great that it left you speechless. Maybe it was an animal or a view on your favorite hike. If you're an artist, you might have a song you find so unexplainably good that you could listen to it on repeat for hours at a time.

I have that awe-filled feeling often.

For me, there's nothing quite like standing face-to-face with a stallion. I'll always remember the feeling I had the first time I met a horse. They're so large and powerful, yet timid and kind. Weighing in at about a thousand pounds, often with rich and full manes, horses are *majestic*. When I look at a stallion, I understand that my power is insignificant compared to this animal's. But there is One who is even more majestic than even the most amazing creature on earth.

God is majestic. His presence is filled with glory, and His works are wonderful.

There's something so awe-inducing and glorious about God that you can't help but fall on your face at the sight of Him. The Bible tells us God's presence is so amazing that we *can't* see Him fully here on earth. God says that *no one* can see Him and live (Exodus 33:20)! The Bible does, however, record several men catching glimpses of God, and they *all* were stunned at His presence.

When Jesus came to earth, He performed wonders and miracles, showing off God's power. But He made it clear that the most wonderful and majestic thing wasn't healing the blind man, the bleeding woman, or the ten lepers. His greatest power wasn't raising Jairus's daughter or Lazarus from the dead. God's most majestic miracle was and is forgiving us of our sin (Matthew 9:1–8).

The God who created you and me is mighty. He is power and majesty itself. And He is stronger than anything our minds can comprehend. That can be overwhelming to think about, but the truth is, if God is all-powerful, mighty, and majestic, there's no safer place to be than with Him. Notice the majesty of God and let it lead you to worship. There's no better place to be than in awe of Him.

Further Reading: Exodus 33

- *What does it feel like to know that the God who created you is the most powerful being ever to exist?*
- *What would look different in your life if you fully relied on God's power?*
- *How have you seen majesty displayed here on earth? How does God's majesty compare?*

BECAUSE GOD IS MAJESTIC, HE IS WORTHY OF MY WORSHIP FOREVER.

GOD IS OUR HEALER

"He himself bore our sins" in his body on the cross, so that we might die to sins and live for righteousness; "by his wounds you have been healed."

—1 PETER 2:24

God is our Healer.

In Exodus 15, we are introduced to one the names of God, *Jehovah Rapha*. It means "the God who heals." It was first used when God promised the Israelites healing if they obeyed His commands and listened to Him carefully.

Sickness is everywhere. In our hearts, bodies, and minds. All of creation is sick.

Chances are, you or someone you know has been sick. It could just be the annual flu you get in the early winter, but it could be more severe. Maybe your heart feels sick or maybe your mind does.

There is hope though—God promises healing for all His children.

Throughout the Bible, we see healing miracles. Sarah and Hannah's bodies were healed from being unable to have children. Naaman was healed of leprosy. Job was healed from the boils that made his life miserable. And Jesus continued to bring more healing: He raised people from the dead, healed the sick, and gave sight to the blind, just to name a few. He still does this today.

Still, healing may not always look like what we imagine. God didn't revive my mom, even though we prayed He would. If I'm being honest, it took me a long time to accept that. In time, though, I learned that He offered her the greatest healing of all: life forever in a new creation with Him.

God may not remove the cancer from your friend's body, and He may not fully remove depression and anxiety from your mind. But He *can*.

Even simply being in the presence of God is healing. Whether you're walking with Him, talking with Him, or worshiping Him, just being around God is medicine to our souls.

Healing doesn't always mean being cured here on earth. Sometimes healing ultimately looks like going to be with God, which we'll be graced to experience eternally one day.

Whether you've personally seen it or not, God is a healer. He is always restoring. God has the power to revive our hearts, our bodies, and our minds. Have you asked Him for that?

Further Reading: Matthew 8:15

- *Where do you need healing?*
- *Do you believe that God can heal you? Why or why not?*
- *What does it mean to you that God* is *healing?*

BECAUSE GOD IS OUR HEALER, I CAN TRUST THAT HE IS ALWAYS HEALING, EVEN IF IT DOESN'T LOOK LIKE WHAT I THOUGHT IT WOULD.

God Is Able

Then the word of the Lord came to Jeremiah: "I am the Lord, the God of all mankind. Is anything too hard for me?"

—Jeremiah 32:26–27

With God, anything is possible. And I mean *anything*. From creating the universe and everything in it out of nothing to parting an entire sea so that hundreds could walk through it to healing the blind, deaf, and paralyzed, God has proven there is nothing He cannot do.

Have you ever waited for a miracle?

I have. My cousin has been injured for a while. As an accomplished athlete and personal trainer, there's nothing she feared more than being unable to use her body. One day, in the middle of a simple sprinting drill, she turned the corner and collapsed to the ground. Her entire body went numb for two minutes. As feeling rushed back to her body, she knew something was wrong. To this day, she needs a miracle.

I've been praying continually, but things look glum. My faith has been tested, and in my darkest moments, I find myself wondering if God is able. Is He just embellishing when He says He can do anything?

If you've felt this way, you are not alone. Still, I'd like to remind us of the truth.

God's Word tells us that *nothing* is too hard for Him. He created everything you see. He tells the breeze when to blow and the leaves when to fall. The Bible is filled with accounts of His ability to do the impossible. Not once has God been overwhelmed by a task. Not once has He wondered if He could accomplish a job. Power is in God's nature, and we can believe He is able because of that power.

Right now, I am praying for a miracle for my cousin. I *know* God is able, and I'm praying that He will help me believe in His ability, that He will display His power through my cousin, and that we will all trust that He is still good even if He doesn't.

What are you praying God will do?

Believing is scary. Trusting that God can do *anything* feels crazy! Whether He answers your prayers with "Yes," "No," or "Not Yet," God is good and able to do anything—even when it feels like our prayers are going unheard. Pray for the impossible, and watch as He writes the greatest story you'll ever tell.

FURTHER READING: MARK 10:27

- *What feels impossible in your life right now?*
- *Do you believe God can do that impossible thing?*
- *What is one small step of faith you can take today?*

BECAUSE GOD IS ABLE, I CAN TRUST THAT IF IT'S BEST, HE WILL MAKE IT HAPPEN.

God Is Just

Righteousness and justice are the foundation of your throne; love and faithfulness go before you.
—Psalm 89:14

God is just. All His ways are fair, and He is righteous—the definition of right.

There's nothing worse than the feeling I get when I see injustice. My stomach turns, and my nose flares. I hate to see people mistreated, and I hate it when things are unfair. By the time I was five, my parents had worn out the phrase, "Life's not fair."

This was so hard for me to understand. Sometimes, it still is.

My desire for life to be fair now is less about the toy I wanted or the fact that my parents got to stay up late while I had to go to bed. It now looks like wishing everybody was born with equal opportunity. Wishing everyone got to have loving parents and a safe home. That seems *fair* to me.

The way I feel when I see injustice isn't random; it's rooted in God's justice. God is just, and He hates injustice more than I do.

The Bible repeatedly tells us that God is just and values justice. Micah 6:8 tells us one of God's commands. He *demands* that we act justly, love mercy, and walk humbly. God is righteous, and He hates it when things are wrong!

Because of sin, life is filled with injustice. We see people do bad things, sometimes without consequence. Horrible things happen. Evil is everywhere, and so is injustice. This is our reality.

But all things *will* be made just again. God promises this. His promises to repay evil and right all wrong. He promises to expose darkness and bring justice to those who have been wronged. Because of God's power, we get to see some of that on earth now. But one day, we will see all of it. When Jesus comes back to restore the earth, He will bring justice with Him, because He is a just God.

While we're here, we get to be vessels of God's righteousness. Everywhere we go should be marked by God's zeal for what is just and love for those He has made.

Embody God in your pursuit of justice. He has clothed you in righteousness. Act justly, love mercy, and walk humbly with Him.

Further Reading: Micah 6:8

- *Where have you seen injustice?*
- *What does God have to say about it?*
- *How does knowing that God will always provide justice make you feel?*

BECAUSE GOD IS JUST, I CAN BELIEVE THAT ONE DAY, THINGS WILL BE FULLY MADE RIGHT.

God is King

On his robe and on his thigh he has this name written: KING OF KINGS AND LORD OF LORDS.

—Revelation 19:16

God is King over all things. He holds lordship over everything you see because He created it, and He owns it all.

There's a Taylor Swift song I used to secretly sing called "King of My Heart." It's got a windows-down-on-a-summer-car-ride vibe. The words, however, aren't ones I would want to be caught singing in public. Mainly because the king she's talking about isn't the one I want ruling my heart. For that matter, neither is any king from this world.

But that's the thing—although God is King over all, He has given us free will. He lets us decide who we want to be in this world and whom we will treat as our king. Though our decision doesn't change His kingship, God allows us the freedom to submit to Him as our King or not.

God created each of us as people with personalities who choose different things. It's one of the things that makes us diverse and beautiful. Our differing tastes in fashion and music or our ability to say "yes" or "no" is all because God gives us choice. But if directed the wrong way, our choices can lead to harm. In the garden, Adam and Eve chose to sin, and without God, our hearts are deceitful and wicked (Jeremiah 17). In our fallen state, our hearts are dark. They can't see what's best for us like God can. We tend to choose to be ruled by popularity, our dating lives, our friendships, how many brand names we own, money, and more.

It doesn't have to be this way. We don't have to stumble around, wondering what to worship. The enemy would love for you to believe your heart is stuck the way it is, but here is the truth: There is a King, and He has invited us into His kingdom.

When God is King over our hearts, He lives in us through the Holy Spirit. Because God is Light, He helps us see that Jesus is the only way to find true contentment. Our hearts go from rotten and deceitful to filled with His love and truth.

God is King. When you recognize that, and step under His rule, you can experience real trust. You can set your worries aside because you know who is in charge. That shame you carry around as if it's part of you will fade away because the *King* has called you daughter. When people think of having a king, they often think of being held down. But life with God as your King is the truest freedom you'll ever experience.

Further Reading: Psalm 47:2

- *Who is the king of your heart?*
- *Who should be the King of your heart and why?*
- *Would you like for God to be King over your life? Tell Him.*

BECAUSE GOD IS KING, I CAN LET GO OF ANYTHING I PLACE BEFORE HIM.

GOD IS HONEST

"And I will ask the Father, and he will give you another advocate to help you and be with you forever—the Spirit of truth."

—JOHN 14:16–17

Nothing stings more than the feeling of betrayal. At some point in our lives, probably more than once, you and I have been lied to or told a lie.

But there is One who can never tell a lie.

God cannot lie. Everything, and I mean *everything*, He says is true.

In John 14, Jesus was preparing the disciples for His departure. Before this, Jesus had spent at least three years walking alongside and teaching these young men. Now, it was time for Him to leave. I imagine panic and fear coursed through the disciples when Jesus told them He would be killed. It would be like your coach or teacher telling you they were leaving. You would be left to figure it out on your own.

The difference is that the disciples' situation was a lot more serious, *and* Jesus didn't leave them to figure it out on their own. Jesus told the disciples He would give them a Helper, the *Spirit of truth*. (You may have heard the Helper called the Holy Spirit or the Holy Ghost.)

Jesus left us all with a Guide. This Spirit tells the truth at all costs, guides us in truth, and *is Himself truth*. This Spirit was the One who guided men to write the promises of God in Scripture.

- When He promises to protect and guide you, He means it. (Psalm 32:8)
- When He calls you fearfully and wonderfully made, He is telling the truth. (Psalm 139:14)
- When He says you were created for a purpose, He isn't lying. (Proverbs 16:4)
- When He tells us He will use all things for the good of those who love Him, He keeps that promise. (Romans 8:28)
- When He reveals that He has overcome the world, you can trust that Jesus has. (John 16:33)

This world is filled with lies, and so are our hearts. But when we invite Jesus into our lives, we receive a Helper—the Spirit of truth. When you don't know where to go, what to do, or whom to trust, remember what God says: He is Truth, and so is His Word. Get quiet and still before God and ask the Holy Spirit to guide you in truth. What a relief. In a world filled with lies, Someone is honest.

Further Reading: John 1:14

- *What do you know about the Holy Spirit?*
- *If the Holy Spirit lives inside of you, how do you notice Him reminding you of truth?*
- *How should the Holy Spirit affect the way you live?*

BECAUSE GOD IS HONEST, I CAN FULLY TRUST HIS WORD.

ALL-KNOWING

*This is how we know that we belong to the
truth and how we set our hearts at rest
in his presence: If our hearts condemn
us, we know that God is greater than
our hearts, and he knows everything.*
—1 John 3:19–20

God Is a Seeker

A man was there by the name of Zacchaeus; he was a chief tax collector and was wealthy. He wanted to see who Jesus was, but because he was short he could not see over the crowd. So he ran ahead and climbed a sycamore-fig tree to see him, since Jesus was coming that way. When Jesus reached the spot, he looked up and said to him, "Zacchaeus, come down immediately. I must stay at your house today."

—Luke 19:2–5

God sees everything, from the farthest star in outer space to the tiniest cricket in your backyard. And if He sees all things, that means God sees you. He sees into the depths of who you are. And in those depths, He loves you so much. He says you're worth saving.

Luke 19 introduces us to Zacchaeus. Zacchaeus worked one of the most hated jobs of his time: He was a tax collector. He worked for the Roman government by taking money from Jewish people (his *own* people)!

He had a reputation for stealing money to make himself rich.

Zacchaeus was a thief. He was a sinner and the last person anyone would have expected Jesus, the Son of God, to notice. (On top of that, Zacchaeus was short, which may have been another reason many people looked down on him.) That's why he climbed a sycamore tree to see Jesus when Jesus came to his town—Zacchaeus couldn't see over the crowd.

You can imagine Zacchaeus's surprise when he heard Jesus call out to him.

"Zacchaeus, come down immediately. I must stay at your house today," Jesus said.

In Zacchaeus's effort to *see* Jesus, *Jesus saw him*. I can almost *feel* the shock that ran through Zacchaeus's body when Jesus peered up and called him by name. I'm sure he was startled and all sorts of confused. Why would Jesus take the time to recognize a sinner like him?

Can I tell you something?

You and I aren't far off from the reality of Zacchaeus's story.

In our sin, Jesus sees us, and He *still* calls us by name. Even if you've never said His name aloud, He knows yours. Better yet, He is calling you. His Spirit wants to live in your heart and make you more like Jesus. Closer than the deepest friend is our all-knowing, all-seeing God who sees you. And He loves what He sees.

Further Reading: Luke 19:9–10

- *How does it feel to know that God sees all of you—even your sin?*
- *When was the last time you wanted to hide from God? What made you feel that way?*
- *How can you remind yourself that you have a Savior who sees all of you and still wants you to come into His presence today?*

BECAUSE GOD IS A SEEING GOD, I CAN TRUST THAT I AM FULLY KNOWN.

GOD IS PATIENT

The Lord *is compassionate and gracious,*
slow to anger, abounding in love.
—Psalm 103:8

God is patient. He is not easily angered, and He operates out of love.

It took me a long time to learn this. I'm still learning.

It's safe to say I'm stubborn. My parents would tell you I thought I knew best at three years old. And as I grew, I continued to think I knew best. (Silly, I know.)

But then I grew up and left home and . . . I still thought I knew best!

It took a few years and some big mistakes to realize that maybe I didn't know everything (anything), but maybe Someone else did.

When I finally called on God, I sheepishly waited for Him to laugh or punish me for my pride and ignorance. I was unexpectedly surprised by His response. As I looked through His Word, I found that God is compassionate and gracious, slow to anger (Psalm 103:8); that He longs to be gracious to me (Isaiah 30:18); and that His patience leads to salvation (1 Timothy 1:16). God patiently guided me in the right direction, mentioning nothing about my past, because Jesus had already taken on the punishment for any wrong I had done.

As humans, we are often slow to learn and slow to listen. Good thing we've got a patient God.

God is aware of our imperfections. He knows our weaknesses, and He knows the deepest longings of our hearts. He knows when we need more instruction, and He always wants to help us. He's the best teacher we'll ever have.

When you find yourself hiding from God or wishing you could understand something sooner, remember who your Father is. He's God. He is patient, and He moves gently and intentionally because He loves you.

Ask Him for help. I have a feeling He'll joyously lead you toward Himself.

Further Reading: 1 Corinthians 13:4

- *Are the adults in your life patient? What do you notice in or about the most patient people in your life?*
- *How do you feel knowing that God is patient with you?*
- *If God is patient with us, how can we be more patient with others?*

BECAUSE GOD IS PATIENT, I DO NOT HAVE TO FEAR THAT HE WILL GIVE UP ON ME.

God Is Jealous

"Do not worship any other god, for the Lord, whose name is Jealous, is a jealous God."

—Exodus 34:14

God is jealous. The first time I heard this, I thought, *That doesn't sound right*. But it's true.

Jealousy is often viewed as wrong. You may have been told, "Nobody likes a jealous girl," or, "Jealousy looks bad on you." And for us, this is true. To be jealous or envious of someone else's achievements or life *is* bad. It's unloving and makes us feel awful.

But God's jealousy isn't the same. God doesn't envy your achievements or what you have. He has and is everything—more than you or I could ever imagine. God's jealousy is different.

Throughout the Bible, one thing upsets God more than anything else: His people turning away from Him and toward something else.

In the book of Exodus, God freed the Israelites from slavery to the Egyptian people. God chose Moses to lead the Israelites out of slavery, and God performed many miracles to free them. In Exodus 32—shortly after He freed them—the Israelites decided to build a golden calf to worship. It was an idol like the idols the Egyptians worshiped.

God hates idolatry—the worship of anything other than Him. God is the one and only God. To put anything above Him is idolatry.

In today's world, most of us don't build altars. We don't pray to golden calves. But we do put things above God. From sports to shopping to achievements and relationships, it can be easy to forget that God is the highest.

God is jealous for our love, our praise, and our attention. He is worthy of all our praise. He wants us to love Him more than anything else because He is the most worthy of love. He desires our hearts, and we need Him. He is the only place our hearts can find fullness.

Remember who created you and who is worthy of your highest attention. No one else deserves your worship. There is no achievement in your sport that will satisfy.

No designer outfit will fill a hole in your heart. There isn't a friend or boy who will make you feel complete. God knows that He is the only one who can satisfy you, fill your heart, and give you a real purpose.

Further Reading: Exodus 32:7–8

- *In your own words, what does it mean that God is jealous?*
- *What are a few things you're tempted to put above God?*
- *How can you lay those things down so you can put God first?*

BECAUSE GOD IS JEALOUS, I CAN FULLY GIVE MY HEART TO HIM.

GOD IS WISDOM

Oh, the depth of the riches of the wisdom and knowledge of God! How unsearchable his judgments, and his paths beyond tracing out!

—ROMANS 11:33

God always knows what to do. He is overflowing with wisdom.

Life is confusing. Sometimes my mind is like a sounding board of differing opinions and facts, with one side of my mind firing off alongside the other. People often tell us opposite things too, and we may feel like we *barely* know who we are. An influencer is telling us one thing while our friends say another. Our parents give us advice that contradicts our teachers. And all the while, it feels like everyone is telling us who we should be.

It can feel like no matter how hard we try, we don't know how to make the right decisions. From college to friendship to determining our identities—it's hard to know what to do and who we are. The world is noisy, and knowing who to listen to is almost impossible. It's overwhelming, to say the least.

There is One who is not overwhelmed though.

God is wisdom. He knows all things, does only good, and acts out of His knowledge and goodness. He makes decisions based on His perfect character, and He wants to help us become more like Him as we deal with complex situations.

I've needed wisdom countless times in my life, and God is the only true source of it. God's wisdom is readily available through His Word and time with Him. Wisdom doesn't just come overnight; it comes when we humble our hearts and ask for God's help. Proverbs 9:10 says that the fear of God is the beginning of wisdom. When we understand who God is, we take the first step toward walking in His wisdom.

Over the next few years, you will have a lot of decisions to make. As you walk through them, remember it's not always about making right or wrong choices; it's about asking God to guide you. God is more concerned with *who* we are than *what* we do, so if we want wisdom and God is wisdom, we should ask God to make us more like Him.

If you haven't already experienced this, you'll soon realize how black and white life *isn't*. But that's exactly what God has answers for. His wisdom guides us in the grey.

When you don't know what to do, look to God. He has all the answers, and He will never lead you astray. Spend time with Him. Collect wisdom from the Bible. Watch as that wisdom takes root in your heart and guides you in the right direction—toward Him.

Further Reading: James 1:5

- *In which area of your life do you need God's wisdom?*
- *What does the wisdom of God sound like in your life?*
- *How can you tell the difference between the wisdom of God and the voices around you?*

BECAUSE GOD IS WISE, I CAN TRUST THAT HIS INSTRUCTION IS BEST.

God Is Our Guide

He guides the humble in what is right
and teaches them his way.
—Psalm 25:9

God is our guide. He knows exactly what we should do and where we should go—*always*.

I think about that a lot because I love to travel. Traveling makes me feel more alive than anything else. My favorite place I've visited is a small country in Africa called Rwanda. It's gorgeous, and from the people to the views to the food, the culture is one of the most beautiful I've ever experienced. I loved all ten of my days there and am itching to go back.

My favorite part of my time there was the safari. I saw giraffes, all kinds of monkeys, hippos, and even elephants up close. It was awe-inducing, to say the least.

However, there were a few moments when I felt unsure. I'm a city girl from Dallas, Texas. Although I was amazed by the different creatures standing just yards away from me, I was also a bit freaked out. Our guide would creep *awfully* close to powerful lions and enormous elephants—with us in the vehicle! I had no reference for how far away we should stand from these majestic beings or what the proper protocol was for interacting with them.

Despite my concern, the guide was unmoved. He mostly ignored my unsure comments and questions because he was confident in what I was not. He had done this thousands of times, and he knew exactly what to do and how to do it.

Life can feel a lot like riding down a rugged dirt road, stumbling across giant creatures and aggressive predators. It can feel scary walking in uncharted terrain, but there's no need to fear. God is the greatest guide you'll ever have, and He's already guiding you.

Our Guide knows exactly what to do. He doesn't just have experience; He has exclusive wisdom because He is the Creator of it all. Long before we were born, God knew exactly who we would be and where we would go. He's already got the map. We must simply follow His directions.

Life may scare you, excite you, or give you questions and doubts. Don't take your eyes off our Guide. God leads from peace, so follow His calm. God guides in confidence, so walk tall. God knows all, so keep trusting Him. And God is guiding you, so follow close. Buckle up for an incredible journey, because the Guide is going to take you on an adventure.

Further Reading: Psalm 32:8

- *Do you trust God to be your guide? How do you show that?*
- *How have you seen God guide you?*
- *In what areas of life do you need God's guidance right now?*

BECAUSE GOD IS MY GUIDE,
I CAN FOLLOW HIM.

GOD IS CREATIVE

In the beginning, God created the heavens and the earth.

—GENESIS 1:1 CSB

My husband and I love road-tripping. We often take out our olive green, decked-out SUV and explore the country. Some of my favorite drives have been up the California coast and through the Pacific Northwest. I love the way the huge trees stake their place in the ground, branches swaying at the smallest breeze. They're so big! Most of the time I find myself staring *up*, trying to take in the beauty of it all.

When I'm out there, I feel inspired. My hands itch to paint the sunset on the water. My voice longs to sing when we drive up the beautiful coast of California.

My creativity comes alive when I'm surrounded by God's creativity. *He* inspires me. Because we were made in His image, His creativity lives in us.

God is the original artist. Before da Vinci or Picasso was God. He meticulously crafted the waters and planned exactly how the waves would hit the shore. He created each of us with different looks, features, heights, and complexions. He created all the different hair textures too! God made *everything* you see around you, and He gave people the ability to create, and He did both with careful intention.

We often think about God's strength and power, but it's easy to forget about His creativity. Jeremiah 10:12 reminds us that His strength, wisdom, and artistry all work together: "But God made the earth by his power; he founded the world by his wisdom and stretched out the heavens by his understanding."

God is imaginative. He is original. If you want to get to know Him, look at what He's made. What does the ocean say about who He is? What do the mountains reflect about His character? When you look at yourself, what does your image tell you about God?

The waves of the sea display God's power. The mountains speak to His greatness. And your image tells of His intricate and meticulous care for His art. From the roots of your hair to the way your nose crinkles when you laugh, God designed you as His best art.

Let God's creativity inspire and awaken your heart. Let His beauty remind you to dream. Create paintings or equations or whatever God has laid on your heart, knowing He paved the way. You reflect Him with your creativity.

Further Reading: Genesis 1:31

- *Do you consider yourself creative? Why or why not?*
- *If God is creative and you bear His image, then so are you. What does creativity look like for you?*
- *Where in God's creation do you go to be inspired?*

BECAUSE GOD IS CREATIVE, I CAN LOOK TO HIM FOR INSPIRATION.

EVERYWHERE

"Am I only a God nearby," declares the Lord, "and not a God far away? Who can hide in secret places so that I cannot see them?" declares the Lord. "Do not I fill heaven and earth?" declares the Lord.

—Jeremiah 23:23–24

GOD IS WITH US

"The virgin will conceive and give birth to a son, and they will call him Immanuel" (which means "God with us").

—MATTHEW 1:23

God is with us. Did you know that?

In the Old Testament, God promised His people (the Israelites) that a Messiah would come to rescue them. Their sin separated them from God, and they needed a Savior. Not only did God promise a Messiah to His chosen people, but He also promised the Messiah would save people from every nation. The Messiah's name was Jesus. He also was called Immanuel, which means "God with us."

This was the first time God's people had God "with" them physically. This baby boy had been born to *be* with His people. Jesus was a depiction of the goodness and grace of God, and He changed our lives forever. Thirty-three years after His birth, Jesus died on a cross, defeating death and resurrecting from the dead so that we could have everlasting life with Him. And then He sent the Holy Spirit to be with us. Galatians 4:4–6 says, "But when the set time had fully come, God sent his Son, born of a woman, born under the law, to redeem those under the law, that we might receive adoption to sonship. Because you are his sons, God sent the Spirit of his Son into our hearts, the Spirit who calls out, '*Abba*, Father.'"

Hundreds of years later, Jesus's death still bears the same weight. Without Him, we would never get to be with God, and the Holy Spirit couldn't be *with us* today.

We might not have been there for Jesus's birth, death, and resurrection. However, what Jesus did for us means just the same as it did back then. When you believe that Jesus died on the cross for your sins and rose again so that you could have eternal life, God can be with you. And a day is coming when we will physically be with Jesus again.

Until that day, His Spirit lives inside of us. (You can read more about this in the next devotion.) We are never alone. What a beautiful reality! For the rest of our lives and into eternity, God will always be with us, and He will never leave or forsake us.

If God is with you, that should affect the way you live. The way you walk. The way you interact with those around you. If God's Spirit is in you, you don't ever have to fear. If God is with you, you will never be alone. If God has made your heart His home, you can *rest*. You are in good hands.

FURTHER READING: DEUTERONOMY 31:8

- *Have you asked the Holy Spirit to live in you? What was that moment like?*
- *Do you trust that God will never leave you? What makes it hard to believe that sometimes?*
- *How does God the Son coming to earth to be with His people make you feel?*

BECAUSE GOD IS WITH ME,
I CAN TRUST THAT I AM NEVER ALONE.

God is in you

And in him you too are being built together to become a dwelling in which God lives by his Spirit.

—Ephesians 2:22

God is in you. Think of your heart as a home.

When you accept Christ as your Savior, He comes into your heart. His Spirit "indwells" you (Romans 8:9). The Spirit of God is powerful and captivating, and He has the power to change you from the inside out.

But just like in any friendship, you have the power to host Him or not. You can cultivate your friendship with Him or forget about Him, allowing His voice to go quiet. Either way, He's there, gently reminding you that He isn't going anywhere.

I grew up in church. I don't remember a day I didn't know God. I always believed He was my Savior, and I knew that He loved me. However, I remember many days when I forgot God was there or didn't care that He was within me. He was always in me, but I didn't listen or talk to Him.

Maybe you've felt the same. Maybe you grew up in church and have known God your entire life. He may have been with you as long as you can remember, but along your journey, you've forgotten Him. You've grown so used to Him being there that you forget to listen for His voice.

God lives *in* us, but that doesn't mean we always act like it. In such a noisy world, it can be easy to forget about Him. As we grow up, the sound of His voice may feel like it's growing faint. We try to shrink His role in our lives, and we only call on Him when needed. We forget to kindle the friendship. We forget that because He lives in us, *He* should change how we live.

What a waste it would be if you had the key to life living inside of you but never did anything with it. If a treasure sat in your house but you never opened it, how foolish would that be? The Holy Spirit has so much to give to you, so much to show you, and has said so much to you through God's Word. God's Spirit is in you—how much would your life change if you lived like that's true every single day?

Don't grow numb to the crazy reality that you have access to God. That is a miracle given to us because of

His grace. If God lives in you, your life can change. It can look radically different from before. Because of God dwelling inside of you, the way you treat others and speak to your parents can be completely different. His Holy Spirit gives you the power to say yes to God every day—to love as He loved, to help when you're confused, and to guide others in wisdom. Don't let His presence in your heart feel dusty; rather, let it make you new.

Further Reading: Romans 8:9

- *What does it mean to you that if you are a follower of Jesus, you have the Spirit?*
- *How much access does God have to your heart? Have you let Him in fully?*
- *If God lives in you, what in your life needs to change?*

BECAUSE GOD IS IN ME,
I CAN ALWAYS ACCESS HIM.

God Is Celebrating With You

The Lord has done it this very day;
let us rejoice today and be glad.
—Psalm 118:24

God is celebrating you! He loves to make it known when things go well. He loves a good reason to throw a party, and He loves it when you join Him in His kingdom work! God is not afraid to dance and sing.

If you had told me in fourth grade that God loved celebrating, I wouldn't have believed you. I went to a Christian school where we went to chapel twice a week, said prayers throughout the day, talked about God, and sang hymns. I learned that God was holy, perfect, and good, but I couldn't tell you much else. The God I learned about seemed somber, quiet, and old.

But can I tell you something? God loves a good celebration. He wrote it into the Law!

Leviticus 23 tells all about it. For each victory the Israelites had in the Old Testament, there was a celebration to remember it. Like our Christmas or Easter celebrations, the Israelites had holidays that they celebrated monthly.

The Passover was an annual feast celebrating the Israelites' liberation from Egypt. The Feast of Unleavened Bread memorialized the Israelites' escape from slavery. The Feast of Tabernacles was the seventh and last feast God commanded the Israelites to celebrate, remembering the forty years of wandering in the wilderness. That's right, God *mandated* celebration!

All the celebrations we see in the Bible, point to one thing: remembering God for what He has done and basking in the freedom that exists because of Him.

God loves celebration so much that He commands us to do it often. Joy is in His being. There is so much to celebrate because there is so much God has done that we must remember. Our lives are to be built on celebration and remembrance.

The best part about God's celebration is that it can be done at any time. In fact, our souls especially need celebration when things are hard. One of my favorite examples of this is in Philippians 1 when Paul praises God from *prison*. He rejoices at the good news of Christ's name being spread. As he was held captive because of persecution, he kept his spirits high by remembering what God had done.

Life will not always be easy, but by remembering what God has done, we are reminded of what He will still do. Celebration is a feast for our souls, and He is with us in our celebrations.

Further Reading: Philippians 4:4

- *Does celebration come naturally to you? Why or why not?*
- *What do you need to celebrate that you haven't taken the time for yet?*
- *How can you embody God's celebratory character this week?*

BECAUSE GOD IS A CELEBRATOR, I CAN TRUST THAT HE REJOICES WITH ME.

God Is Mourning With You

He was despised and rejected by mankind, a man of suffering, and familiar with pain. Like one from whom people hide their faces he was despised, and we held him in low esteem.

—Isaiah 53:3

God mourns with you. When you are so sad that you don't know how to pray, the Bible says His Holy Spirit prays for us with "wordless groans" (Romans 8:26). The Bible also says that God the Son is deeply acquainted with pain, grief, sorrow, and suffering.

None of it is foreign to Him. When God the Son came to earth as Jesus, He suffered. He died. He experienced mental torment and physical pain. He is called the Man of Sorrows. Jesus experienced the same sad emotions you do. He can mourn with you because He knows your pain.

In John 11, a man named Lazarus, a friend of Jesus, was sick. His sisters, Mary and Martha, sent word to Jesus that their brother needed healing. Jesus received their message, and after a few days, He went to Lazarus, knowing His friend would already be dead. Sure enough, by the time Jesus got there, Lazarus had been in the tomb for four days.

Imagine being one of Lazarus's sisters—the hopelessness and despair you'd have felt in that moment. Maybe you don't have to imagine. Maybe you've felt it.

When Jesus arrived, Mary fell at His feet. She wept and cried out, "Lord, if you had been here, my brother would not have died" (verse 21). As she wept, so did the others who were there. The Bible says that Jesus was deeply moved in spirit and troubled. And then Jesus did something surprising.

Jesus wept.

Rather than swooping in and hushing their tears, Jesus connected with their pain. He cried too. He felt their sorrow and hopelessness and was moved to tears. In the end, Jesus did heal Lazarus, but He didn't rush the healing. He didn't skip past the sting of death. He fully sat with those who were hurting and hurt *with* them.

Even now, the Holy Spirit prays for us, with our pain. He is not in any rush to skip past your grief. Though sometimes, God allows your pain, but He never shames your sadness. His Spirit is moved by your tears. When you feel sadness, pain, or the sting that comes with sin and death, you are never alone. God has been grieved over sin, death, and their effects long before we have, and one day, He will take them away. Until then, God is mourning with you, catching your tears alongside His own.

Further Reading: John 11:35

- *What's the most painful thing you've ever walked through?*
- *Looking back, how do you know that God walked with you through it?*
- *How does it feel to know you're not alone in your grief?*

BECAUSE GOD MOURNS, I CAN TRUST THAT HE IS WITH ME IN MY GRIEF.

GOOD

Give thanks to the
Lord, for he is good;
his faithful love
endures forever.
— Psalm 107:1 CSB

God Is Good

The Lord is good to all; he has compassion on all he has made.
—Psalm 145:9

It's not supposed to be this way.

You don't have to live a long time to realize that this world is dark and often forces hard situations on us.

It's *not* supposed to be this way.

I was introduced to the pain of unthinkable loss the summer of my ninth-grade year. It felt like our family was at its strongest: We were moving states for my dad's exciting new job. My mom was advancing in her career, and my sisters and I felt nothing but loved and cared for.

Within hours, a large and looming storm cloud enveloped my whole world. My life went from joy to sadness when my mom suddenly died. The world as I knew it collapsed.

I don't know what your storm cloud looks like, but I know you've got one. Whether it came with tragic news, crippling anxiety, an accident that wrecked your world, or painful memories worming their way into the deepest parts of your mind and making a home for themselves, we are all familiar with the messed-up ways of the world. But tragedy and death are not God's good design for earth.

When God created the earth, there was no darkness, pain, sorrow, or loss. God's design was fully good because God is fully good (Genesis 1). There is no higher standard for goodness than God. He is the very definition of good (Luke 18:19). A few chapters after the creation of the world, sin entered through man. And because of sin, death, darkness, and pain were ushered in too.

But God, in His goodness, didn't leave us alone in our sin. He is our Refuge, our safe place. When we experience the unthinkable, He's closer than we can imagine. God grieves alongside us, and because He is good, He doesn't stop there. Romans 8 tells us that God uses all things for the good of those who love Him.

There is hope for your story, both here on earth and when God comes back to make all things fully good again—even better than the original design.

It's not supposed to be this way. And because we serve a good God, it won't always be.

FURTHER READING: ROMANS 8:18–30

- *What hard thing have you experienced that causes you to question God's goodness?*
- *Do you tend to invite God into your pain or to shut Him out?*
- *What would change if you believed that God is working all things for your good?*

BECAUSE GOD IS GOOD,
I CAN TRUST HIM.

GOD IS LIGHT

God is light; in him there is no darkness at all.

—1 JOHN 1:5

God *is* light.

As a kid (and even into adulthood if I'm being honest), sleeping at night was hard. Something about the darkness was ominous and scary. I'd lie awake for hours, waiting for the sun to rise. As soon as I saw a sliver of light, my anxious mind would ease, and my body would fall into a deep sleep.

I remember having one of these episodes a few years ago. I laid awake as a grown adult, waiting for the sun to rise. I felt vulnerable and afraid. The darkness of the night was overwhelming.

Suddenly, the Holy Spirit reminded me of something: God *is* light.

It was like He said, "Lena, I am the sun you are waiting for. And I shine *always*."

God is the light your soul longs for. God is *always* light.

Because we live in a broken world, everything is tainted by darkness. Our worlds, our hearts, and our minds are all dark. The good news is that we don't have to stay in the darkness. God sent His Son, Jesus, to die for our darkness and to offer us His light. Because of Jesus, we can live *in the light*.

Maybe our tendency to fear the dark is deeper than that of a child being afraid of a black room. Maybe our fear of physical darkness speaks to how opposite it is to God's character.

God is as bright as the sun. Brighter actually. Everything is revealed in and through Him, and when we are with Him, nothing that can truly hurt us lingers in the shadows. His hope reaches far and wide, and His light beckons you to live a bright and hope-filled life.

When we choose God's light, we do not have to be afraid of the darkness.

Further Reading: Psalm 18:28

- *In what areas of your life do you need to remember that God is light?*
- *How does it feel to know that God is light and there isn't even a hint of darkness in Him?*
- *In what areas of your life do you need to reflect God's light?*

BECAUSE GOD IS LIGHT, I DON'T HAVE TO LIVE IN THE DARK.

GOD IS KIND

"But love your enemies, do good to them, and lend to them without expecting to get anything back. Then your reward will be great, and you will be children of the Most High, because he is kind to the ungrateful and wicked."

—LUKE 6:35

Have you ever had a friend who gave you something beautiful on a random day for no reason? Maybe it was flowers or chocolate. The best gift I ever got for no reason was a gift card to my favorite store. (This girl knows how to shop, and it's even better when it's free!)

God has given us many gifts—without us having to do anything to earn them.

God, holy and perfect, has given us forgiveness and the opportunity to spend eternity with Him. For most of us, He's given us clothes on our backs and food on our plates. He gives beautiful sunsets to watch and crisp fall mornings to enjoy. His kindness is universal, spreading to all, both those who follow Him and those who don't. But God's kindness to His children is special.

I'll never forget when I was on one of my favorite trips, a safari in Rwanda I went on two years after losing my mom. (That was one of God's kindnesses already.) Something special happened on that rugged ride as we weaved between the grasslands of Rwanda and Tanzania. I looked out the window after seeing one of my favorite animals and cried. Silent tears streamed down my face as I longed for my mom's warm embrace. I just wanted to experience this trip alongside her.

As I looked up, wiping my eyes dry and hoping that no one would notice, I saw hundreds of dainty butterflies flying alongside the jeep. It felt like they were driving us along the grassy path. Floating almost.

In seeing the swarm of butterflies, I felt my mom's warm embrace and Jesus's comfort. I didn't do anything to deserve it. He simply saw me crying and was kind.

Have you had a moment like this? At the moment, you might have seen it as "luck" or happenstance, but I can assure you, it was God's kindness. And His greatest kindness? It's that even though we don't deserve forgiveness for our sin, God forgives us anyway. He made a way for us to be with Him again and to experience His kindness for all of eternity.

God loves each of us individually. He knows our quirks, what makes us giggle. What makes us cry. And occasionally . . . or maybe even often . . . He taps into the things that move us just to make us smile.

That's the God you are loved by. Walk in the gift of His kindness. It's chasing after you.

Further Reading: Ephesians 4:32

- *What did you perhaps mistake for luck that you now see as God's kindness?*
- *Is it hard or easy for you to believe that God is kind? Why?*
- *How does it feel to know that God likes making you smile?*

BECAUSE GOD IS KIND, I CAN WALK IN HIS GIFT OF KINDNESS.

GOD IS PEACE

Now may the Lord of peace himself give you peace at all times and in every way. The Lord be with all of you.
—2 THESSALONIANS 3:16

God is peace. It's more than a hand sign you throw up at the middle school dance. We typically think of peace as feeling calm and free of conflict, but peace is actually within the fabric of who God is.

I've been a bit of a nomad for most of my early adulthood. Rather than going to college, I moved back to my hometown, Dallas, Texas. I was there for about a year, and then I moved back to Tennessee. Over the course of a few years, I lived in about five different homes. I'm now married and have a permanent-ish home. But I've always loved the nomadic life.

Or I did until God called me somewhere dark. He called me to live up close with real pain and darkness, and it was scary. I spent six months fighting fear and searching for peace. And then I realized something:

If I have God, I am filled with His peace.

Second Thessalonians says, "Now may the Lord of peace himself give you peace at all times" (3:16). Peace isn't something we find; it's something we *have* in God. When God finds us, we find peace.

David describes peace with God as walking with Him beside still and quiet waters . . . laying in lush green pastures (Psalm 23:2). I have a feeling David was a bit of an outdoorsman.

Where do you feel the peace of God? How do you know He is walking with you? Maybe it's in the car or at your favorite park. It might be in your cozy bedroom or the shower, on a rainy winter afternoon, or a sunny morning at the beach.

We can often become attached to these *places*, thinking God's peace only resides there. And sure, His peace can feel extra close in those places. But if you are walking with God, peace is with you wherever you go.

In the darkest valleys or on the highest mountains, peace is with you, because *God* is with you. Whether you find yourself "nomad-ing" through life in a valley or on a mountaintop, the peace of God is always with you, and you can rest in that.

Further Reading: Psalm 23

- *Where do you most naturally sense God's peace?*
- *What is it like to know that God's peace is with you everywhere you go?*
- *What changes in your life when you remember that God's peace fills you?*

BECAUSE GOD IS PEACE, I CAN HAVE PEACE NO MATTER WHAT MY CIRCUMSTANCES ARE.

God Is Merciful

The Lord *is compassionate and gracious,*
slow to anger, abounding in love.
—Psalm 103:8

God is merciful. So, what is *mercy*?

Mercy and grace are often used synonymously. However, they are not the same.

In the beginning, God created a man and a woman. Their names were Adam and Eve, and they were what God called "very good." Everything about them was exactly how God intended them to be. They had the most beautiful garden to roam about, and they had only one rule: God commanded them not to eat from one tree, the tree of knowledge of good and evil.

Everything was as it should be . . . until it wasn't. A sneaky serpent lied and convinced them they could be like God. They should eat from the tree. They did, and sin entered humanity. God is perfect, and He made us without sin. But when we sinned, we messed that up. God stayed perfect, and we became sinners, completely separating ourselves from Him. The punishment for sin is ultimately death. However, God made a way for us *not* to suffer what we deserve. He didn't immediately kill Adam and Eve, and He even made them clothing to cover them up before they had to leave the garden. But one day, an even better covering would come.

So what is mercy? Mercy is *not* receiving what we *do* deserve. In that garden, Adam and Eve deserved death, and every human afterward deserved the same thing. Our very existence is a sign of God's mercy. Waking up each day with breath in our lungs is only because of God's mercy.

Our sin condemns us to a life eternally separated from God. This is called hell. And it's what we deserve because our sin keeps us from being with God. But there's hope: God made a way for us to escape eternal death. And not only escape it but also live *forever* with Him. Jesus died on the cross and *covers* us with His righteousness so we can be with God again. *That* is mercy.

The greatest love story ever told is the one where God saves us from ourselves and loves us with a love we do not deserve. Without God, we are destined for eternal darkness. That's what sin gets us. With God, we get to experience His mercy and receive grace: life with Him forever.

God's mercy is what saves us from the punishment we deserve. We deserve death, but God is merciful because He loves us. It's the greatest love story you'll ever hear, and you and I are in it.

Further Reading: Ephesians 2:4–5

- *In your own words, what is mercy?*
- *Where have you seen God's mercy displayed in your life?*
- *How should the mercy of God impact how you live?*

BECAUSE GOD IS MERCIFUL, I DO NOT HAVE TO FEAR PUNISHMENT.

GOD IS GRACIOUS

For it is by grace you have been saved, through faith—and this is not from yourselves, it is the gift of God—not by works, so that no one can boast.

—Ephesians 2:8–9

Grace is defined as the "free and unmerited favor of God." While mercy is *not* getting the punishment we *do* deserve, grace is *receiving* something good we *don't* deserve. After mercy, *grace* is God's gift to us. We don't deserve it, and there's nothing we can do to earn it, yet God gives it freely.

Growing up, we had one big dinner-table rule: You must eat your food before doing or having anything else. My sister and I would sit at the table until we finished every bit of our sweet potatoes or squash, or [insert your least favorite vegetable here.] "Happy plates" were what we called a cleared plate. Most of the time, I'd make it to a happy plate. But occasionally, the texture of squash would just be too much for me, and I'd revolt.

On those rare occasions, my parents would usually give me grace. They'd allow me to leave the table and join in on a delicious treat, despite my unhappy plate.

This is like what God gives us, but what He gives is much better. Our unhappy plate is our sin. And the yummy treat we receive is eternal life. But in God's story, Someone took the punishment we deserve for our "unhappy plates": Jesus.

We are sinners. You and I, no matter how hard we try, are broken, and our hearts are wicked. We don't deserve any of God's good gifts. We deserve death. Our sin, on its own, separates us from God. His holiness cannot come close to the unholy and unrighteous state of our hearts.

But God, in His love for us, loved us so much that He gave us grace. His Son paid the price for our sins and gave us the best gift we'd ever receive: salvation.

God sent His Son to die for us. Jesus took on the weight of our sins and paid the ultimate cost so that we could spend forever with Him.

God's grace, His unmerited favor, and His kindness are written all over our lives. Do you have air in your lungs? You have been given grace. Do you have people you love? Grace. Do you have God? Grace. The grace of God is why you and I are still here. The grace of God is why you and I have hope. The grace of God is intertwined in our stories. And ultimately, the grace of God is what saves us from our sins and gives us life with God forever. We are all proof of the love and favor of God.

FURTHER READING: ROMANS 5:20–21

- *Where can you see God's grace in your life?*
- *Since you've been given grace by God, where can you extend that grace to those around you?*
- *What does God's grace mean for where you will spend eternity?*

BECAUSE GOD IS GRACIOUS, I GET TO SPEND ETERNITY WITH HIM.

God is Sanctifying You

May God himself, the God of peace, sanctify you through and through. May your whole spirit, soul and body be kept blameless at the coming of our Lord Jesus Christ.

—1 THESSALONIANS 5:23

When we walk with God, He makes us more like His Son. God is continually sanctifying us.

Sanctification is a big word, but it is simply the process of being freed from sin and made more like Jesus. It's what our life journey should consist of, but it's only possible through the Holy Spirit.

Growing up, though, I thought that if I tried hard enough, read my Bible long enough, and didn't say bad words, I would make myself "sanctified." It wasn't until I hit high school that I realized sanctification is a lot more complex. It has nothing to do with my performance.

When sin entered the world, it should have been the end for us. We were bound for hell because our sin separated us from God.

There is good news though. God loved us so much that He made a way—through Jesus, His Son—for our sin to not to have the final say. Through Jesus, we can be saved from sin's punishment and spend eternity with God. In the meantime, sanctification is how God makes us more and more like Jesus.

Sanctification is not the tasks you do to follow God, but what the Holy Spirit does in your heart throughout your life. It's when a Bible verse convicts you to stop gossiping or when tragedy strikes and the Spirit teaches you to rely on God. It's when you notice that you are praying without having to think about it.

I don't know your story, but it's safe to say you've made one or two (or ten million) mistakes. You might believe you are beyond repair. You might even believe your mistakes define who you are for the rest of your life.

But God calls us blameless. Jesus has paid for our sin, and His Spirit gives us the ability to say *no* to sin and *yes* to God, even though we still live in a broken world. We don't have to carry the weight of our sin any longer, and we get to become more like Jesus.

But God didn't just call us blameless and then leave us alone. No. He calls us blameless and walks with us, molding us into who He made us to be. That is sanctification.

God says you are not beyond repair. And what God says is true. Join hands with Him and walk out your God-given sanctification. You don't have to do anything special or complicated to receive this gift. You are His child. You already possess it. Watch as God pieces you back together and shapes you into all that He designed you to be. God loves you, and He loves sanctifying you. He loves helping you become who He made you to be.

Further Reading: 1 Corinthians 6:11

- *What mistakes have you made that you have believed define you?*
- *What does God say about your identity in light of your mistakes?*
- *What has sanctification looked like in your own life?*

BECAUSE GOD IS SANCTIFYING ME, I CAN TRUST THAT I'M BECOMING MORE LIKE HIM.

PROMISE
KEEPER

For no matter how many promises God has made, they are "Yes" in Christ. And so through him the "Amen" is spoken by us to the glory of God.
—2 Corinthians 1:20

GOD IS TRUSTWORTHY

Abraham answered, "God himself will provide the lamb for the burnt offering, my son." And the two of them went on together.
—GENESIS 22:8

God is worthy of our trust. His promises are always true, and obedience to Him requires us to trust Him. But we're conditioned to be skeptics. How could we not be? The world is filled with lies. To walk around trusting everyone or everything would be silly. So when the Bible tells us to trust God—full stop—that feels scary.

No man knew that fear better than Abraham. God used Abraham to start the nation of Israel—God's nation. God promised He would make a great nation from Abraham and his wife, Sarah, and their many, many children.

One problem: Abraham and Sarah had never been able to have kids, and they were *old*—too old to naturally conceive. They often struggled to trust God fully, but they trusted that God would keep His promise. They prayed for a son for years. Sure enough, Sarah gave birth to their son, Isaac, at the age of ninety.

Then in Genesis 22, God told Abraham to take Isaac—the *same* son God had promised and whom they labored over in prayer for years—up to a mountaintop to offer him as a sacrifice to God.

Now, if God telling Abraham to kill his son weren't crazy enough, Abraham and Sarah had prayed for Isaac for decades! Moreover, God had promised Abraham that he would be the father of many through Isaac's line. How did killing Isaac line up with that promise?

But Abraham trusted God and obeyed. Why? Abraham had a history with God. He believed that God would provide and that God was trustworthy. Abraham remembered *Who* gifted him with all that he had: God.

The story ends well. God gave Abraham a ram to sacrifice at the top of the mountain instead of Isaac. He was testing Abraham's trust. He wanted to give Abraham an opportunity to act out his faith—to prove that he really believed in God's promises (Genesis 22:12).

God won't ask you to sacrifice your child as a burnt offering, but God may require significant trust from you. Maybe you're aware of God's power but wonder why He allows bad things to happen. You might not know God very well yet. Trusting Him feels like putting faith in a stranger.

As you grow with God, you will see that He is trustworthy. God had promised that a great nation would continue through Abraham's son, Isaac, and Abraham trusted that God wouldn't break that promise. In fact, Hebrews 11:19 tells us Abraham believed that *even if* he killed Isaac, God would surely raise him from the dead!

No one is more worthy of your trust than your Creator. God is faithful. His promises are trustworthy. And His love for you is greater than you could ever imagine.

Further Reading: Genesis 22:1–18

- *What has your experience with trusting God looked like?*
- *Do you believe that God is trustworthy? If not, what's stopping you?*
- *What area of your life do you need to trust God with?*

BECAUSE GOD IS TRUSTWORTHY, I CAN TRUST THAT EVERYTHING HE SAYS IS TRUE.

GOD IS FAITHFUL

Jesus Christ is the same yesterday and today and forever.
—HEBREWS 13:8

God is faithful. He is unchanging and loyal to the end. God keeps His promises, is always steady (unlike us), never leaves, and is constant in His faithful love toward you.

I admire baseball fans. They're die-hard fans. I've never cared for the game, but I can't deny that sitting in the crowd with a giant hot dog at the Texas Rangers, stadium is electric. The best part, though, is watching everyone else's excitement for the game and love of their teams.

I can't name one player, but I can tell you all about my friend who has rooted for the same team and player her *entire* life. Her family never misses a game no matter wins or losses, successes or failures. Now *that* is some faithfulness.

If you were to multiply their faithfulness and love by infinity, *that* is how God feels about us and every one of

His children. Since the day we were born, God has been present. He pursued us by sending His Son to die on the cross for our sin and to make us a part of His kingdom. He keeps chasing us by giving us the Holy Spirit, who helps us follow God more closely. And He is always with us—at every recital and game, every bedtime and breakfast. God hasn't missed one. This is faithfulness.

The best part is that nothing we do enhances how "big" God shows up for us. His steady love and faithful presence are there just the same. Can't remember the last time you picked up your Bible? That's okay; God is still faithful. Struggling to find the words to pray? All good; God is still faithful. Been struggling with the same sin you just can't seem to break? God is faithful and will not leave your side.

We live in a flaky world. We're often let down by others, and everything is always changing. People, places, circumstances, and rules seem to transform almost weekly. But God never changes. He is faithful, even when we're not. He is the *one* constant in our lives. When everything else fades, He will still be our faithful Father, Friend, and Guide. He's not going anywhere. When you feel anxiety welling up inside, remember who your Father is. He's constant. Faithful. Steady. He's showing up for you, day after day. Take His hand, and rest in His faithfulness. Take a deep breath. He is never going to change.

FURTHER READING: 2 THESSALONIANS 3:3

- *Have you been surrounded by faithful people? What is it like to have faithful friends?*
- *How is God's faithfulness different from what you've experienced with people?*
- *How does God's faithfulness make you feel?*

BECAUSE GOD IS FAITHFUL,
I CAN REST IN THE FACT THAT
HE WILL NEVER LEAVE ME.

GOD IS HOPE

May the God of hope fill you with all joy and peace as you trust in him, so that you may overflow with hope by the power of the Holy Spirit.

—Romans 15:13

God is hope. He is the only reason we can expect or desire good. He is the reason we can look up and say, "Maybe next time." If we are His, we have a sure future. Without God, we would be hopeless and trapped in utter misery.

Depression is rampant in our world and is growing by the day. If it's not you, someone you know and love is probably battling it, and I am deeply sorry. A lot of factors go into why we might experience depression, but regardless of how we get there, it stinks. If you've woken up with zero desire to live, you are not alone. (And please tell someone you love and trust. Then ask a parent or loved one to help you find a licensed therapist, biblical counselor, or medical doctor.) If thoughts of darkness have ever taken over your mind, you are not alone. And if you just feel sad or deeply unhappy, you're not alone either.

I've walked alongside friends with chronic depression, and I've walked through bouts of depression while grieving my mom's death. I know how hard it can be, and how utterly hopeless you may feel. Here is some truth: We have a God who operates out of hope, and His hope holds weight in all our lives. God knows the hope you need. He knows that things are not the way they are supposed to be.

Isaiah 53:3 says God is acquainted with grief (see page 105). And He has promised us it won't always be like this. Revelation 21:4 tells us that God will "wipe away every tear" from our eyes. He promises that death will be no more. He tells us we won't cry or mourn. *This* future with God is what gives us hope.

Life won't be this way forever. One day, when Jesus comes back to restore the world as He promised, all pain will disappear.

If you are deeply sad or hurt and feel hopeless, pray that God will help you remember you are not without hope. You may not *feel* hopeful, but this world isn't forever. God is coming back to restore our minds, our hearts, our bodies, and our souls. He will make everything new and right. If you have God, you have hope for a future. Even when you don't feel it, it's there. Thank God for His kindness in giving us hope—we couldn't live without it.

Further Reading: Isaiah 40:31

- *In your own words, what is hope?*
- *Do you have hope? Has there ever been a time when you felt hopeless?*
- *How does the hope of God help you live?*

BECAUSE GOD IS HOPE,
I CAN LEAN ON HIM WHEN
MY HEART FEELS DISCOURAGED.

GOD IS FORGIVING

If we confess our sins, he is faithful and just and will forgive us our sins and purify us from all unrighteousness.

—1 JOHN 1:9

God does not hold grudges or past mistakes over our heads. He *wants* to forgive us and make us clean, and nothing you can do will undo His forgiveness.

Have you ever messed up big? Growing up, I was a bit self-righteous. I'd make mistakes but never what I considered "big ones." For years, I wore my goodness as a badge of honor and pride. When I got older, I couldn't keep the facade together. I started to mess up. I made *big* mistakes. It wasn't that I hadn't made mistakes in the past; it was just that others could now see them.

I felt the shame that sin often brings. For months, it tangled itself into my identity, and I convinced myself that my sin made me far from God. I confessed over and over and over, but the shame wouldn't go away. As a follower of Jesus, I knew God had forgiven me, but in my heart, I thought, *How could He ever want to forgive someone like me? Surely, I've blown it by now.*

This is the lie that the enemy wants us to believe—that God doesn't want to forgive us or that He won't. When Satan gets into our heads, we start to believe that we are without God and that He doesn't love us.

This couldn't be further from the truth. The Bible says there is "*no* condemnation for those who are in Christ Jesus" (Romans 8:1, emphasis added). When we believe in Christ, we are freed from the punishment of sin that we deserve. Rather than wagging His finger at us as we sink into shame, God forgives us and makes us clean—not because we did anything to earn it but because, when He looks at us, He sees His Son, Jesus.

We are new in God's eyes, thanks to Jesus's death and resurrection. God has forgiven you—past, present, and future. It is finished.

If you've been tormented by the fear that God hasn't forgiven you, or that He has taken His forgiveness away, recognize the lie. Because God forgives us and gives us the Holy Spirit to guide us, we can recognize our sin and turn toward Him. No matter how big or small you may have messed up, you are washed in God's grace. You are pure in His sight. He holds no grudges and longs to make you clean, so let Him!

Breathe deep. You are clean.

Further Reading: Matthew 6:14–15

- *How hard is it to ask God to forgive you?*
- *Do you believe God forgives you? Why or why not?*
- *How should God's forgiveness toward you affect how you treat others?*

BECAUSE GOD IS FORGIVING,
I CAN LIVE IN FREEDOM AND KNOW
THAT I AM CLEAN IN HIS EYES.

GOD IS OUR ROCK

The LORD is my rock, my fortress and my deliverer; my God is my rock, in whom I take refuge, my shield and the horn of my salvation, my stronghold.

—PSALM 18:2

When you walk around, do you sometimes feel like difficult things is coming at you from every angle? Do you feel the weight of the world bearing down on you?

Study how your body feels—where is the tension? Chances are that your shoulders are tight and your knuckles tense.

It makes sense.

The older we get, the more our responsibilities stack up. In our homes, schools, friendships, and lives, we have a lot of obligations—projects due, places to be, and people who need us. It can be weighty, exhausting, and anxiety-inducing. Maybe a voice in your head is saying you can't do it all. Or perhaps the temptation to sin comes in from every angle, from the internet to peer pressure to our desires inside. It may feel like you can't escape—like there's no place to hide.

I walked around like this for years. (I sometimes still do.) I've been overwhelmed by the load of responsibilities and lies from Satan always weighing on me, and I've been discouraged and ashamed when I messed up or missed the mark.

It's not that I had it worse than anyone else. I just didn't realize I have a place to hide, and that I can't handle it all on my own. I have Someone strong to shield me from every threat. When David wrote this psalm, a rock was considered a tool of war, something to hide behind to shield the attacks of the enemy.

God is our Rock. He is reliable, strong, calm, and our biggest support. God can handle what we can't, and we can trust our lives in His hands.

We don't carry our responsibilities or escape temptation on our own. You and I have a giant, sturdy Rock to hide in. When the going gets tough or the odds stack up high, God is there for us. We can rely on Him. He can shield us from anything, and nothing will crush Him. He is our refuge!

God our Rock can hide us from the weight of the world. So walk around confidently, knowing that the Rock covers you. When you are tempted to fear the things coming your way, remember that He is protecting you. Let the weight go to Him. He can handle it. Because God is our Rock, we can rely on Him.

Further Reading: 2 Samuel 22:32

- *What do you feel weighed down by?*
- *When you feel like the temptation to sin is everywhere, what can you pray?*
- *What does it tell you about God that He is your rock?*

BECAUSE GOD IS MY ROCK, I KNOW HE IS COVERING AND PROTECTING ME.

SAFE PLACE

Fear of man will prove to be a snare,
but whoever trusts in the LORD is kept safe.
—PROVERBS 29:25

God Is Our Refuge

God is our refuge and strength, an ever-present help in trouble. Therefore we will not fear, though the earth give way and the mountains fall into the heart of the sea.

—Psalm 46:1–2

God is our Refuge. He gives us shelter and protection. He promises to protect us through the worst of storms, and He tells us not to be afraid. He is ever-present, meaning He is *always* here, and He watches over us with vigilance. Even the mountains and waves bow down at the sound of His voice (Psalm 46:6).

Over the course of less than five years, four people in my family died: my mom, my uncle, my aunt, and my great-grandfather. One after the other, people I loved disappeared at a rate faster than I could handle. I was sad, confused, and so many other emotions at once. Along with feeling the typical grief that comes with such huge losses, I felt anxious. I became unsure of myself and the safety of those around me. I imagined what it would feel like to lose someone else, and the fear of another loss began to overtake me.

If we're being honest, life often feels overwhelming. Whether it be fear of the future, literal danger all around us, or just small things piling up, it can feel like there is good reason for anxiety and fear.

However, God tells us the opposite. Psalm 46 tells us the truth of who God is: our Refuge and our Help. When we know who He is, we don't have to fear! Joshua 1:9 tells us not to be afraid because God is with us wherever we go. In Isaiah 41:10, God tells us not to fear because He is with us. And 2 Timothy 1:7 declares that God has not given us a spirit of fear but a spirit of peace, love, and a sound mind.

God knew we would struggle with fear, and He wanted to make it clear that fear and anxiety are not our burdens to carry. God does the heavy lifting for us. He doesn't need our anxieties or worries to do His job.

Thankfully, God didn't let me be overtaken. In the night-time, when I was most afraid, I knew God was with me. I could feel His presence close beside me, often holding me on the floor of my bathroom as I sobbed. God was with me every step of the way as I learned that I could rest in Him.

As a recovering worrier, I know it's not easy to quit. It doesn't even feel natural at first. But God is our Help, no matter the trouble. He's fighting for us and providing shelter all at the same time. Tonight, today, wherever you may find yourself, trust in His words. He is our Refuge, so we need not fear.

FURTHER READING: 2 TIMOTHY 1:7

- *What has your journey with worry looked like? Are you a natural worrier?*
- *What does it feel like to know that the God of the universe is always your Helper?*
- *In what areas of your life can you throw off worry and embrace the truth that God's got it all in His hands?*

BECAUSE GOD IS MY REFUGE, I CAN CONFIDE IN HIM WHEN I AM AFRAID.

GOD IS OUR PROTECTOR

So do not fear, for I am with you; do not be dismayed, for I am your God. I will strengthen you and help you; I will uphold you with my righteous right hand.

—Isaiah 41:10

When you give your life to God, He will send you to some scary places, but He will never send you somewhere without His protection.

What do you think of when you read the word *protection*? I used to think of protection in the same way as I did my bedtime teddy bear. As a child, if I thought I heard a scary noise or imagined a shadow in my closet, I'd grab ahold of my stuffed animal and squeeze it as tight as I could, like it could keep me safe from the monster under my bed. But that stuffed animal didn't work for long.

After a couple of minutes, my imagination would run wild. I'd sprint out of my room to shake my dad awake, knowing his arms would be the only place I'd feel safe. It's hard to explain the feeling of his tight squeeze as I my breaths slowed down, and I was lulled back to sleep.

Feeling safe is something we all long for, but as we grow older, it's less realistic to wake up Dad, Mom, or an older sibling.

Recently, God sent me to some scary places. I longed for a stuffed animal or a big strong dad to hold me once again. I didn't realize I had something even better. The darkness felt consuming, and I couldn't imagine staying in the fear much longer.

I cried out to God, begging for help. He gave me the strength to take one day at a time and to stop being so scared. Eventually, He released me from my scary situation. And guess what? I was still in one piece—still whole.

God will send us to all kinds of places, from hospital rooms to dark home lives. You see, when God promises protection, He doesn't always mean He'll keep us away from danger. Most times, He calls us *to* darkness and hard places for the sake of others and to be made more like Jesus. (After all, didn't Jesus put Himself in harm's way for us?) But God's promise of protection means that in danger, true darkness cannot touch us. He will keep our souls alive. He will protect us from the only thing that threatens *real* danger: eternal death.

We can walk into battles because God will keep us intact. We might fall. We might scrape a knee. We might even experience real, physical harm. However, we will not be alone. God comes with us. God promises to protect us. And He keeps all His promises.

Further Reading: Psalm 91:3

- *Do you struggle with fear? Fear of what?*
- *How does God's promise of protection make you feel?*
- *What are some scary places where you need God's protection?*

BECAUSE GOD IS MY PROTECTOR, I CAN TRUST THAT HE WON'T LET ANYTHING DESTROY ME.

GOD IS OUR COMFORTER

Praise be to the God and Father of our Lord Jesus Christ, the Father of compassion and the God of all comfort, who comforts us in all our troubles, so that we can comfort those in any trouble with the comfort we ourselves receive from God.

—2 CORINTHIANS 1:3–4

Do you ever wonder where God is in your season of *hard*?

What season of *hard* are you in right now?

In the thick of it?

On your way out of it?

Waiting for it to hit?

I remember asking that for an entire year when I was fourteen and grappling with my mom's death. I would often think, *Surely God was supposed to be here and wasn't.*

He and I wrestled for months. Actually, it was more like I wrestled with Him.

Where is He? I wondered. The answer is easy to see now.

He was holding me.

God doesn't promise to prevent life's pain. We live in a fallen world, tainted by sin, so pain is inevitable. God does, however, promise to be our comfort in the pain. It breaks His heart as much as it does ours when we experience hard things.

I don't know what season you're in, but I know that you've either been in pain or are in pain right now. Whichever it is, God is holding you. He is the God of *all* comfort. That means He is better than any earthly comfort you could receive. Are you fighting His embrace? Or resting in it?

Whether your season is hard or whether you are preparing for the hard to come, let God hold you. Receive His deep rest. He doesn't need you to stop crying before you sit in His arms. He doesn't even need you to be okay with the fact that He didn't prevent the pain before you go to Him. All your feelings are okay to take to Him.

Much of my story is marked by pain, which means it's marked by God's comfort too. And as God calls me to walk closely with those whose stories are also woven with pain, I can offer the same comfort I received from God. Because God comforts me, I can comfort others. So can you.

You *can* feel true comfort on some of the hardest days of your life. When you stay close to God, you'll learn so much about who He is. He may answer some of your questions. He may calm you in your fear. But most of all, He'll give you comfort. It's what we all need.

Further Reading: Psalm 23:4

- *What hard things do you need God to hold you through?*
- *Does anything prevent you from resting in God's comfort? What is it?*
- *What can you do to start believing that God's comfort is better than anything else?*

BECAUSE GOD IS MY COMFORTER, HIS LOVING ARMS ARE BETTER THAN ANYONE ELSE'S.

GOD IS OUR LISTENER

"But when you pray, go into your room, close the door and pray to your Father, who is unseen. Then your Father, who sees what is done in secret, will reward you."

—Matthew 6:6

God hears you. He hears every word you've ever spoken, thought, or felt.

My sister grew up feeling a little overlooked in our family. She was smack in the middle of a crew of four sisters, and she often felt unheard. (To me, of course, she seemed the loudest. Now I understand she was just making sure someone heard her.) We were raised by incredible parents. *Great* doesn't even begin to describe them. They loved and cherished each one of us and would never purposely ignore any of us. However, pecking order can take over, and middle children can end up feeling overshadowed and misunderstood.

But there is a parent who never misses a word that one of His children says—God. God is the only One who always hears you and always knows what you're trying to say. No matter your birth order or life story, He is listening. And guess what? The gospel—God's good plan to rescue us through Jesus—makes this possible.

In the Old Testament, God's presence rested in a holy temple. It was found in the innermost part of the temple—the "Holy of Holies"—and a veil separated what lay in that room from everything else. God is holy and man is not. In fact, God is so holy, it would have been dangerous for an unholy person to enter.

But Luke 23 tells us that when Jesus was crucified for our sins, that veil was torn in two. The separation between man and God was broken, and eventually, the Holy Spirit—God Himself—came to dwell in the hearts of everyone who has faith in Jesus. Because of Jesus, Christians can always be in the presence of God.

Maybe you are shy and don't feel comfortable adding your thoughts to a conversation. Maybe you are confident in sharing what you think and need, but no one seems to be paying attention. As humans, we crave a listening ear. We want to feel understood and heard. Our Creator made us this way, and He is the only One who can truly fulfill that desire.

God's listening ear is better than that of a good parent or amazing friend. When He hears you, He never turns away. When you call out to Him, He is listening—intently. He is always present. He loves the sound of your voice; He is the One who gave it to you. You can stop fighting to be heard because God always hears you. Rest in the fact that your Father in heaven is listening. What will you tell Him?

FURTHER READING: PSALM 66:17–20

- *Consider a time when you felt misunderstood. What made you feel this way?*
- *When was the last time you cried out to God?*
- *What do you want God to hear you say?*

BECAUSE GOD IS A LISTENER, I CAN SPEAK FREELY TO HIM, KNOWING HE HEARS ME.

GOD IS CARING

Cast all your anxiety on him
because he cares for you.
—1 PETER 5:7

God cares. He cares about you, your circumstances, the people you love, and so much more. He cares more deeply than any friend ever could. He is the One who looks after you, the One who fills your needs.

Have you ever been second best? Maybe it was on a team or in a friendship. Maybe you feel like the second choice in relationships or even in your family. Not feeling like a priority can hurt. It wears at our esteem and tears us down. From not getting picked for the game in gym class to being the lone wolf in a room of hundreds, it all stings.

But even if we were picked first or had the biggest friend group, our hearts still wouldn't be satisfied. We were created for a deeper kind of care.

In Matthew 8:2–3, a man with leprosy approached Jesus. At that time, leprosy was almost any skin disease that caused visible sores or severe damage to the body. It was also believed to be highly infectious. People with this condition were considered unclean outcasts. They couldn't go sacrifice or worship at the temple. And if they touched anyone, they would not only potentially spread the disease but would also make the other person unworthy to go to the temple.

But when the sick man approached Jesus and asked for care, Jesus didn't flinch. You see, the man asked to be made "clean." Rather than simply declaring the man healed or turning away as the man approached Him, Jesus *touched* the man.

Jesus's care for this man was so deep that even the scariest of diseases couldn't turn Him away. The man's uncleanness didn't transfer onto Jesus; Jesus's holiness transferred to the man, and he could go be in God's presence at the temple!

God's heart for you looks the same. He cares so deeply for you that He sent His Son to jump into the human mess, and because Jesus's holiness transfers to us, we can have a forever relationship with God. God's care is deeper than anything we can understand, and right when we think we understand the depths of His care, we see another layer of it.

When God created you, He knew you'd need Him. He planned to care for your soul, and He does—gladly. Not only does God care about you, but He also gives the same care to all His children.

How much better could it get?

Further Reading: Matthew 8:2–3

- *How does it feel to know God cares for you?*
- *What in your life do you have a hard time believing God cares about?*
- *Since God cares for you, what can you trust Him with?*

BECAUSE GOD IS CARING, I CAN TRUST THAT EVERYTHING HE DOES IS GOOD.

GOD IS OUR HOME

Lord, you have been our dwelling place
throughout all generations.

—Psalm 90:1

God is our forever home. When we don't have anywhere to go or we feel unsafe, God is the safest oasis. Though our earthly homes are often chaotic, He is peace. God makes our hearts His home. If we have Him, He is with us, and we are home.

I've always admired people who live in the same house their entire lives. I had a friend whose grandmother lived in the same place throughout her life, and I got to spend some time there too. The smell and warmth made it the homiest place I'd ever been. I gravitated toward it. One summer, I spent almost two months at my friend's home, swimming in the backyard pool.

I've craved this kind of consistency my entire life, but my life hasn't been that consistent, well, ever.

We moved around regularly when I was growing up, and I loved the excitement of a new house and a new city.

I always had my family—my true home when the other things around me kept changing. But there were parts of the inconsistency I didn't like. Like my mom dying and having to make new friends in an entirely new city with one of my parents suddenly gone.

When she died, I felt homeless. And honestly, for the next couple of years, that feeling stuck around. I searched for a home in other people. In boys, in friends, in my own family. None of those things satisfied what my heart craved. I wrestled with fear and worry and wished my life were consistent and predictable, like my friend's grandma's house. I realize now that I was searching for home.

Eventually, I realized I had a home, and His name is God.

God is a home for anyone who follows Him. He is consistent and steady. He is safe, and His character is unchanging. People come and go, and homes change. But God stays the same. He is the home our souls crave. He has always been, and He will always be. For the rest of eternity, He is our home—the safest place we could ever know.

This journey of life is just beginning for you. You will endure significant change. Things will feel out of control sometimes. Even you will change, and that can be scary. But remember that you have a home in God. He is *the* home. He is *the* safe place. In Him, you can rest.

FURTHER READING: PHILIPPIANS 3:20

- *How would you describe your home?*
- *What does God's home feel like?*
- *How can you regularly remind yourself that God is your home?*

BECAUSE GOD IS MY HOME,
I CAN TRUST THAT I AM SAFE
NO MATTER WHERE I GO.

GOD IS OUR FATHER

A father to the fatherless, a defender of widows, is God in his holy dwelling.

—Psalm 68:5 CSB

God is the perfect Father. He is a Father to those without one, and He fills in the holes our earthly fathers may have missed . . . and then some.

I don't know what your dad is like. You might know him, and you might not. You might be close to him or distant. No matter what role he's played in your life, it's safe to say he's a fallen human (which means he isn't perfect).

So much of our lives are shaped by how we see our fathers. From the way we view ourselves to the way we view other men, our dads shape a lot of that. But how different would our lives be if we saw God as our first Father?

You have a perfect Dad—the One who knit you together before anyone knew you (Psalm 139:13). The One who knew your name before anyone else did—even your parents who named you. The One who's been watching and protecting you since before you were born. You've got the best Father ever, and He's not going anywhere.

It's crazy to think about God loving me more than my dad does, but it's true. You are God's daughter, crafted together by His hands and uniquely placed in this world at this particular time. When God made you, He knew exactly what He was doing, and there isn't a day He wishes He had done anything differently.

He loves *you* more than even the most loving person on this earth ever could.

He . . .

- protects you
- leads you
- provides for you
- is always there for you
- will never fail you

Whether you've got an incredible earthly dad or one who might have a bit of work to do, you *do* have a Father. And He's the greatest One you could ever have. His love for you reaches far and wide. He cares for you like no one else. He protects and supports you better than the best dad you could imagine.

God is your Father, and He is glad to be. His children make Him smile. Rest in His fatherly embrace today.

FURTHER READING: ISAIAH 63:16

- *What is your relationship with your dad like?*
- *How does it feel to know that God is your Father?*
- *How does knowing that God is your Father affect the way you live?*

BECAUSE GOD IS MY FATHER, I CAN TRUST THAT HE LOVES ME LIKE NO ONE ELSE CAN.

LOVE

And so we know and rely on the love God has for us. God is love. Whoever lives in love lives in God, and God in them.

—1 John 4:16

GOD IS LOVE

Whoever does not love does not know God, because God is love.

—1 John 4:8

God is love. He is the embodiment of love. And His love is true. Before God created you or me or anything, He existed as the Trinity—one God in three persons (see pages 19–21). And at the heart of God's nature is love. The Father has forever been pouring out His love on the Son through the Holy Spirit. The triune God has always been the definition of love.

But now more than ever before, the word *love* can mean a lot of things. It's been thrown around, used up, and made to be less than it is. Love can often seem shallow, ingenuine, or even hypocritical. So many people have done evil things in the name of "love." Love can feel confusing. But it shouldn't be.

We have a blueprint for love in the Bible. God's Word shows us what love truly is, and the magnitude of it should overwhelm us. John 15:13 tells us that the greatest form of love is sacrifice, to lay down one's life for another. This means that the greatest form of love took place when Jesus laid down His life for *every single one* of us.

When sin separated us from God in Genesis 3, that broke God's heart (Psalm 78:40). He loves us so much, and He wants to be with us, but His holiness can't engage with our sin. The only way for Him to be with us was to take on our humanity and die in our place, defeating sin, death, and hell.

And God did this. He sent His Son, Jesus, to die a brutal death so that we wouldn't have to be separated from Him forever. Hebrews 12:2 tells us that, "For the joy set before him, he endured the cross." God loves us so much that His Son willingly, joyfully sacrificed Himself for us. *That* is love.

People may have told you they love you, and yet they let you down. They betrayed you. They were selfish. They lied or stole from you. And maybe you've done the same. We've all failed to love at some point because we aren't capable of true and pure love.

God has never failed to love you. Everything He has ever done for you has been out of love because He *is* love.

When you find yourself searching for love or trying to figure out whom to love, remember the truest form of love: the perfect God who came to earth as a man to die a death that you deserved because He loved you.

He loves you, and His love is perfect.

FURTHER READING: 1 CORINTHIANS 13:4–8

- *What has your experience with love looked like?*
- *Do you believe that God loves you?*
- *How will the truth that God is love affect how you live?*

BECAUSE GOD IS LOVE,
I CAN TRUST THAT EVERYTHING
HE DOES IS DONE OUT OF LOVE.

God Is for You

What, then, shall we say in response to these things? If God is for us, who can be against us?

—Romans 8:31

God is for you. He delights in you and is on your team.

What has your support system looked like? You may have been loved and cherished since day one. Your teachers and friends have cheered you on through everything, and your parents see nothing but the best in you.

But maybe your story is more complex. Perhaps you've felt unwanted, or it wasn't until later that you found a support system. Maybe you're still searching for that kind of care. Perhaps a divorce, a friend's harsh words, or something else has gotten in the way of you feeling fully loved. You have never known someone who truly had your back. If that is you, I'm sorry. Regardless of your earthly support system, I want you to know that you've got a better supporter than anyone could ask for: God. He happened to design the entire universe, form colors and gravity, and create *you*.

God offers His support by fighting against our accuser, Satan. When Satan points out our sin, God sees the perfection of His Son. When Satan tries to shame us, the Holy Spirit reminds us we are free from sin. God does not condemn us. No matter how you've felt cared for in the past, God is *for* you. Everything He does is because of His love for His people. All the things in your life—the good, bad, and ugly—serve a greater purpose that God specifically crafted for you.

There's no better father, coach, teammate, or friend than God. He delights in fighting for you and protecting you, and as one of His precious children, His eyes are on you at all times. He's stronger than any father ever could be, and He gives the love of a mother too.

No matter who's in your support system, God is your advocate. His actions are always *for* you, even if they aren't what you'd choose. He will challenge you to grow and hold you when you feel low. He will protect you and test you so that you grow. He will walk beside you and carry you when you're afraid. Jesus is advocating for you in the heavenly places. Rest. There is no greater love for you than His.

FURTHER READING: PSALM 56:9

- *What does your earthly support system look like?*
- *What holes in your heart would you like to have filled?*
- *How does knowing that God is for you make you feel? Do you trust that He will fill the hole in your heart?*

BECAUSE GOD IS FOR ME, I CAN REST IN THE TRUTH THAT I AM FULLY SUPPORTED, ALWAYS.

GOD IS HUMBLE

And being found in appearance as a man,
he humbled himself by becoming obedient
to death—even death on a cross!
—PHILIPPIANS 2:8

God is worthy of all our praise. He is the center of the universe, our very reason for being alive. He is the greatest, yet He is humble.

Think of your favorite athlete, actor, or band. Chances are, the person you'd define as the "greatest of all time" probably knows it. Do you think Serena Williams doesn't know she's one of the greatest tennis players in history? Do you think Cristiano Ronaldo is unaware of his extreme soccer success? (I may have just outed myself on who my favorite athletes are. Whoops.)

The hardest part about success, fame, or notoriety is that not only do you know how great you are, but everyone else knows it too. If I were the greatest athlete of all time, it would be hard to not be vain. I'd probably have the urge to walk around with a puffed-up chest and a decent amount of pride. I'd be the greatest of ALL time . . . who wouldn't get an ego boost from that?

The truth is, God is the greatest of all time and for all time. But instead of flaunting it or using His power to make us feel small, He humbled Himself. Philippians 2:8 says God the Son emptied Himself by taking on a human nature and going all the way to the cross for us.

Jesus took on the ultimate form of humility. He is God! He had every right to leave us to our own punishment because of what it would take to save us, but He didn't.

He went low so that we can go high. He died so that we can live.

The God of the entire universe is humble. He is the God who created you, me, and the whole universe—the God who formed each star and planet. He is worthy of all our praise, honor, and worship. And He showed a humility we all can imitate.

He walked in our shoes, lowly and meek, all while still being powerful, righteous, and omniscient. He loves us and is willing to get down on our level so that we can experience all His goodness. I can't imagine a better God than the One who loves me enough to lay aside His high position to help me live. There isn't one.

The God who created you is humble, and His example teaches us how to become humble too.

FURTHER READING: MATTHEW 11:29

- *How does it feel to know you were created by a humble God?*
- *Does humility come naturally to you? Why or why not?*
- *How should God's humility impact how you live?*

BECAUSE GOD IS HUMBLE,
I CAN FOLLOW HIS EXAMPLE
AND LIVE HUMBLY TOO.

God Is Sustaining Love

. . . And I pray that you, being rooted and established in love, may have power, together with all the Lord's holy people, to grasp how wide and long and high and deep is the love of Christ, and to know this love that surpasses knowledge—that you may be filled to the measure of all the fullness of God.

—Ephesians 3:17–19

How have you experienced love? When I write that word, do you feel warm inside? Or does the word *love* make you feel cold or bring up fears of betrayal and loneliness? Your view of love can be morphed and twisted by your experiences. Luckily, God's love doesn't morph. It is steady.

God created you, and like any creator, He views you as His beloved masterpiece.

From your head to your toes, God loves you. His love is better than any father's or friend's. His love is deep, wide, and never-ending, and there is nothing you can do to escape it. God's love is unconditional. You can do nothing to earn it, and you can do nothing to lose it. More than anything, God wants you to know how loved you are, because everything you do will flow from that. God is love, and His love changes, challenges, and sustains us.

God's love changes us. When we know we are loved by God, it impacts the way we view ourselves. Rather than picking apart the parts of us God made, we learn to embrace them the way God did as He created us. We can believe that it doesn't matter what anyone else has to say about us, because we are loved by the most amazing being in the universe.

God's love challenges us. God's love for us reminds us to love others well. When we understand how much God loves His people, our love for others deepens. Knowing what God's love feels like helps us ache for all people to experience that same love.

God's love sustains us. We all want to be loved. When we realize God's love is enough, we can walk securely in the fact that we are *already* loved. And that is more than enough.

God's love is an undeserved gift that each of us receives. His love isn't a stand-offish side hug. God's love is full on. He is running after us, pursuing our hearts so that we will live joyously because of His love. Some of us know we are living in that love, and others of us still need to embrace it as our own.

Accept God's embrace and rest in His love. It is the best love there is.

FURTHER READING: JOHN 3:16

- *How would you define love?*
- *How is God's love different from the way the world defines love?*
- *What changes when you believe God loves you?*

BECAUSE GOD IS LOVE, I CAN TRUST THAT I'M LOVED UNCONDITIONALLY.

GOD IS JOY

You make known to me the path of life; you will fill me with joy in your presence, with eternal pleasures at your right hand.

—PSALM 16:11

God is joy. It's in His nature. God is happy. He rejoices and calls us to do the same.

I've lived a lot of hard. In the span of five years, my family and I walked through multiple deaths of people closest to us. I became deeply acquainted with grief, disappointment, and despair.

I'm not sure what you've walked through, but it's very possible you know despair too. And if you don't, you will. This broken world we live in makes it almost guaranteed.

But that's where joy comes in.

Joy is often considered to be a cheery attitude, but this couldn't be further from the truth. Joy is lasting contentment—no matter what is happening in our lives. Joy is a state of being, not just a feeling, and it can take root even when we don't feel it.

How can it be that I have joy even in despair? It's simple. God is joy, and if we are Christians, God lives in us. Joy is God-breathed into our souls. It's what carries us through trials and what holds us up when we're feeling down. Joy is what we all need in all seasons of life.

Galatians 5 tells us that when we have God's Spirit, we have joy. Joy is a fruit of God's Spirit, and it will naturally grow in us. No matter our circumstances, we can have joy. Paul tells us in Philippians that he had immense joy, even though he was in a Roman prison cell. His circumstances were the definition of hard, but the Holy Spirit gave him a joy that you and I have access to as well.

You will still cry, you will still grieve, and you will still long for the day when hardship is over forever. We weren't meant to live in a state of hard eternally—thank God! One day, He'll make all things new. Until that day, joy can take root in your heart. It won't stop the tears or numb the deep feelings of sadness, but joy *will* carry you through them.

If you're looking for something deeper and longing for something better, joy is available to you. God wants to live in you, and once He does, He will be your joy. His joy is lasting. It is secure. God's joy will ground you during chaos and carry you when you can't walk on your own.

FURTHER READING: JOHN 15:11

- *Think about a time when you had joy even when it didn't make sense. What was that like?*
- *What does God's joy feel like?*
- *How should God's joy impact your life?*

BECAUSE GOD IS JOY, I CAN LIVE JOYFULLY TOO, DESPITE HOW I FEEL OR WHAT MY LIFE LOOKS LIKE.

GOD IS BEAUTIFUL

One thing I ask from the LORD, this only do I seek: that I may dwell in the house of the LORD all the days of my life, to gaze on the beauty of the LORD and to seek him in his temple.

—PSALM 27:4

What is the prettiest thing you've ever seen?

The most stunning thing I've seen was in France. On a whim, my aunt and I decided it was a *great* idea to go paragliding. This was before I realized I was coming down with a monstrous flu and that when you paraglide, you have to run off a cliff. That's right. I, along with my instructor, had to run at full speed off the top of a mountain, achy flu and all.

I took a few deep breaths, collected my thoughts, and just went for it. Running full speed and leaping—I remember the feeling of freedom as the wind hit my back. I was as sick as a dog, but that didn't stop me from being utterly amazed at the view beneath me. It was iconic, but it was nothing compared to the mind that thought that view up: our God.

God's beauty is deep. But deeper than His appearance, His character is beautiful. He created all the beauty in the world, and He is more glorious than anything He has made—prettier than any sunset you've witnessed, song you've heard, or creature you've seen. The beauty all around you is just a glimpse of what God is like.

God's passion and grace, His love and mercy, God's holiness and wrath are *all* beautiful. He has no flaws, no character defects. He is perfection. This makes Him the most stunning thing we'll ever experience.

God's beauty inspires us, but it mostly keeps us in awe. David wrote of God's beauty in Psalm 27, saying all he longed to do was gaze at the Lord's beauty and *dwell* with Him.

God's beauty is invitational. It will draw us in and fill us with awe until we fall to our faces in worship. If we ponder God's beauty in all that He is, we will walk away inspired and changed.

So let's slow down and gaze upon God, let's think about Him and all that He has done, and let's dwell on His character, creativity, and words. We can do this by meditating on His Word, enjoying His creation, singing songs about His glory, or praying and sitting in silence and solitude. It'll be like running full speed into a beauty beyond anything we can comprehend.

Further Reading: Psalm 50:2

- *When was the last time you dwelled on God's beauty?*
- *Where can you see God's beauty in your life?*
- *How does God's beauty impact the way you see the world?*

BECAUSE GOD AND EVERYTHING HE CREATED IS BEAUTIFUL, I CAN PRAISE HIM.

SHEPHERD

The Lord is my shepherd, I lack nothing.
—Psalm 23:1

GOD IS A FRIEND

"You are my friends if you do what I command."

—JOHN 15:14

The best friendships are built on mutual love, respect, and care. Have you tried having a deep friendship with someone who doesn't reciprocate? It can be exhausting. Trying to be friends with someone who doesn't respect you like you respect them or love you in the way you love them can quickly become dysfunctional. The friendship often doesn't work.

I spent my middle and high school years figuring this out—determining what values I could compromise on to be friends with someone. In the end, I realized that all good friendships are built on respect and love. But Jesus says that the disciples are His friends if they obey Him (John 15:4).

But what does that mean? Does God let go of us when we sin? When we have an unholy thought or fall into temptation? Do we have to perfectly obey Him to earn His friendship?

I struggle to make it a full minute perfectly following God. In fact, outside of Jesus's help, we cannot follow God at all.

But do you know who *did* perfectly follow all of God's commands? Jesus. When we accept His sacrifice for our sins, God counts Jesus's perfect obedience as our obedience, and the Holy Spirit helps us. He gives us the option to do what God commands.

It is impossible to cultivate a one-sided friendship. But because God loves His children, He's all-in. He's pursuing our hearts, and He's made a way for us to be all-in with Him too. When we abide in Jesus and obey His words, we deepen our friendship with Him.

When we walk in friendship with God, we grow. We *want* to obey Him more. Friendship with God is like having the wisest, smartest, and most loving best friend all the time. When we cultivate a friendship with Him, the outcome is always us becoming better—more like Jesus.

When we disobey, God doesn't turn His face away or disown us as His friends. He has already counted Jesus's obedience as our own. It is *our* hearts that drift as we choose things other than Him. He doesn't become distant; we do. If you feel distant from God, it's not because

He left you. He's waiting for you to choose Him. Obedience to Him is visible evidence of your heart choosing Him and of the Holy Spirit working in your life.

Pray for God to give you a longing for friendship with Him. Pray that He will open your eyes to what you're missing when you choose other things. He has already chosen you, so pursue friendship with Him. It is the best choice you'll ever make.

Further Reading: Psalm 25:14

- *Are you a friend of God? Why do you say that?*
- *What gets in the way of being friends with Him?*
- *How would embracing your relationship with God affect your other friendships?*

BECAUSE GOD IS A FRIEND,
I CAN ACCEPT HIS INVITATION
TO LIVE IN FREINDSHIP WITH HIM.

GOD IS IN PURSUIT

Now the Lord *provided a huge fish to swallow Jonah, and Jonah was in the belly of the fish three days and three nights.*

—Jonah 1:17

We cannot escape God. We cannot outrun or trick Him. Even when we try, He endlessly pursues us. So much so that if someone tried to run, God might send . . . I don't know . . . a giant fish to swallow them and stop them. In fact, He's done that.

I'm talking about Jonah. You may have heard his story as you were growing up.

God told Jonah to go immediately to Nineveh to announce judgment against its people. In response to God's call, Jonah fled. He didn't like the people of Nineveh. They were *too* sinful. Why should they get a chance to turn toward God?

Jonah found a merchant ship headed to Tarshish, a town in the opposite direction of Nineveh, and hopped on. While Jonah was aboard, God brought a huge wind.

It was so strong that the ship almost broke. When Jonah told the other men the storm was his fault, they threw him into the sea, and the storm stopped. Jonah was then swallowed by a fish and lived inside it for three days. He was given a second chance, and so were the people of Nineveh.

Jonah's story is often used to talk about God's kindness and mercy to Jonah or His patience with Jonah as he tried to outrun God. But I'd like to focus on the craziest part of it all: God sent a fish.

Rather than moving on to another person to fulfill the call God had for Jonah or scolding Jonah into obedience, God let Jonah run. But even in Jonah's running, God didn't stop pursuing him or the people of Ninevah. He sent a storm, then a fish—God was not going to stop chasing Jonah's heart. And He wasn't going to let the Ninevites go without the opportunity to turn away from their sin and toward God.

What kind of person continues to pursue someone who doesn't want anything to do with Him? What kind of person goes to such great lengths to guide someone after they've made it clear they don't want to be guided?

Only a kind Father whose pursuit is so fierce that He'd do anything.

If God did this for Jonah and the Ninevites, who knows what He would do or send for you?

FURTHER READING: LUKE 15:4–6

- *In what ways has God been pursuing your heart all along?*
- *How have you responded to His pursuit of you?*
- *Are you running from what God might be calling you to? Why?*

BECAUSE GOD WILL NEVER STOP PURSUING ME, I CAN FULLY EMBRACE HIS LOVE.

God Is Gentle

You have given me the shield of your salvation, and your right hand supported me, and your gentleness made me great.

—Psalm 18:35 ESV

Did you know that God is gentle? Yes, He is powerful, mighty, and strong, but He is also tender, soft, and meek.

In today's world, we rarely see both power and gentleness displayed at the same time. From one extreme leader to the next, few exhibit the idea of balance. For many presidents, coaches, and business leaders, power is seen as strong leadership. Who has time for gentleness when there are things to do and people to lead?

God does.

Galatians 5 lists gentleness as a fruit of the Spirit. This means that gentleness is embedded in who God is. He is love, He is peace, He is patience, and He is *gentleness*.

In high school, I had all kinds of coaches, teachers, and authority figures. The ones I remember, though, were kind. They were gentle and thoughtful. They didn't use their power to their advantage. Instead, they held it in high regard, knowing the power they had been given was a responsibility.

God is not a power-hungry deity. He has all power, yet He is thoughtful—the gentlest leader you'll ever have. Like a shepherd leading His sheep, He guides us with compassionate leadership. And when He needs to, like a good shepherd, He picks us up and carries us to safety.

Though God sometimes comes to us in big ways—like coming to Job in a whirlwind (Job 31:1–7)—God is often gentle in the way He speaks. His voice can be found in the silence as a whisper or a nudge. He is thoughtful with His words.

God is gentle in the way He moves too. He guides us in the right direction. Like a flock of birds flying on the wind or a slow and steady stream, God's movements are precise and thoughtful. He doesn't act rashly or rush. He doesn't need to.

God is gentle in the way He teaches. God is not quick to be angry or quick to punish. His Spirit brings things to our attention and gives us space to see where we are wrong and need to try again.

If you're wondering what qualities a good leader should hold, look to God. He has all power and is still tender. He doesn't stop being one to be the other. His gentleness gives us the courage to grow and follow His lead. Remember that you have a gentle Father. Listen for His whisper.

Further Reading: Galatians 5:22–23

- *Who is the greatest person you know? What do you notice about their spirit?*
- *How does it feel to know that God is gentle with you?*
- *How should the gentleness of God move you?*

BECAUSE GOD IS GENTLE, I CAN TRUST THAT HE WILL ALWAYS BE GENTLE WITH ME.

GOD IS REST

By the seventh day God had finished the work he had been doing; so on the seventh day he rested from all his work.

—GENESIS 2:2

I'm never late, but I'm always rushed.

God operates out of rest, and in His presence, we find rest.

Every single morning, I overestimate the amount of time I have to get ready for the day. I wake up relatively early, and from the second I open my eyes, my brain is on. Without fail, I sleepily turn to my side and begin jotting down all the things coming to my mind. "Don't forget to do this" or "Make sure you get to that."

Somehow, amid all the running around my brain is doing, I misjudge the time I have. Before I know it, I'm thirty minutes out from a meeting downtown. I clumsily grab all my belongings and rush out the door. I hop in the car, anxiety pounding inside of my chest as I rush out of my neighborhood to somehow make an 8 a.m. meeting that's thirty minutes away . . . at 7:48.

This is me, and if you're anything like me, you understand this feeling.

It took me a while to realize that my morning pattern was dysfunctional and unhealthy at best. When I rush around first thing in the morning, I spike my stress levels before my body is even fully awake. My body and my soul were rejecting this method. Why? Because it's not how we were designed to live.

Our culture tells us that we must always do a thousand things. You must do every activity, or you won't get into that college. Hustle, hustle, hustle, or you won't succeed in that career path. Oh, and by the way, you've got a palm-sized computer in your hand to distract you the whole time.

After God created the universe, He rested. When Jesus walked the earth, not once is it recorded that He rushed or moved hastily. The Bible tells us to come to God, and He will give us rest. It doesn't say, "Come to God and He'll help you get everything done fast." Anxiety, stress, and rushing are all contrary to the way God moves and the way He created you to move.

Rest doesn't always mean taking a nap (although sometimes it does). Living out of rest simply means moving from peace, security, and calm. Because we're human, life won't always feel restful. There will be busy seasons and crazy days, but when we go to God, we can find the rest we need.

Further Reading: Matthew 11:28

- *Why do you think God rests?*
- *Do you operate out of rest? What does that look like in your life?*
- *In your own words, describe why rest is necessary.*

**BECAUSE GOD IS REST,
I CAN FIND MY REST IN HIM.**

GOD IS KNOCKING AT YOUR DOOR

"Here I am! I stand at the door and knock. If anyone hears my voice and opens the door, I will come in and eat with that person, and they with me."

—REVELATION 3:20

God is knocking at the door of your heart because He desires a relationship with you. More than you long to be with Him, He longs to be with you. He celebrates when any one of His children answers His call, and He gladly takes a seat beside you at your table. God wants to be with you.

It can be hard to believe we are wanted.

If you've been to middle school or high school, you know how it feels to wish you were liked. I went to a school where not many people looked like me. I stood out. I was different. My hair was extra curly and my skin extra brown. My difference in appearance was no secret. I had trouble making friends too. No boys liked me, or at least no boys admitted to it. Very quickly, I decided I wasn't wanted.

Social pressure teaches us that our achievements make us wanted by others. If we act like the other girls, speak however our culture teaches us to, and look picture-perfect, we will be desirable. This destroyed my self-esteem. I burned my curly hair straight until it didn't curl anymore. I ate less and less so that my thighs wouldn't rub together when I walked.

I couldn't understand why God made me the way He did. I didn't realize He made me the way He did because *He* loved me. When He made me, He designed me with intention.

No matter our performance or physical appearance, there is Someone who desires us enough to knock at the door of our hearts. He sees us as His perfectly crafted daughters, and He cares about our hearts more than anything else. He *longs* for us, more than we could ever long for anything.

No matter what the world tells you, you are wanted because you are God's. Our identity doesn't have to be wrapped up in the way we look or what any person thinks. We have a God who went to great lengths to pursue a relationship with us, His children. What more could we need?

The God of the universe wants to spend eternity with you. If you are His child, you get to live in light of that truth forever. The most powerful, important being to ever exist sees you and wants you. God desires you, and that is more than enough.

Further Reading: 1 Timothy 2:3–4

- *Have you ever felt unwanted?*
- *What does it feel like to know that you are wanted by God?*
- *What changes in your life when you remember that you are wanted, first and foremost, by God?*

BECAUSE GOD DESIRES ME, I CAN TRUST THAT I AM ALWAYS WANTED.

God Is Holding You

Yet I am always with you; you
hold me by my right hand.
—Psalm 73:23

God is holding you in His hands. He knows your every move before you do, and He knows every feeling you've ever had. He knows the way your heart aches and the things that light you up. He knows when you lie down and when you wake up. And He holds it all. He holds you, your heart, and your future in His hands.

It's been six years since I've had the hug of a mother. It's been six years since I was held by *my* mother.

My mom, Wynter Pitts, died six years ago. Since then, I've longed to be held by her. As I prepared for a wedding, marriage, and a new season, all I wanted was to be held by my mom.

I wanted to sit in her lap, although we'd be the same size now. I longed to lean into her as she detangled my hair or scratched my back. The warm embrace only a mother can give. It was all I wanted but could not have during that season.

I cried out to God and asked Him why. Though I didn't hear Him audibly answer my questions, I was held. *He was* the One holding me. When I cried, He held me. And when I questioned His goodness in my life, He never let go of me.

And it's not just in the hard parts of life that God is nearby. He's held me since the very beginning—since before I lost my mom. His embrace is the warmest one I'll ever receive, and His comfort is all I need. In our pain and grief, in our joy and excitement, God is holding us.

He doesn't fill the holes in our hearts with the love of those we miss; rather, He fills them with love that is so much better.

God knows the nuances of our lives. He knows our pain. He knows the absences and losses. He sees our longings, and in everything, He holds us.

He's holding our future. He's holding our past. He's holding our feelings. He's holding our brokenness with the truth that, one day, He will restore us.

God is holding you and giving you comfort. His embrace is warm and long. He is your Shepherd; His comfort is never-ending. He is big enough for every part of your story.

Further Reading: Isaiah 46:4

- *Consider a time you longed to be held. How can you look back and see that God was holding you the whole time?*
- *What does being held by God feel like?*
- *What holes in your heart do you need God to fill?*

BECAUSE GOD IS HOLDING ME,
I CAN REST IN THE FACT THAT
HE WON'T LET ME GO.

GOD IS OUR HELPER

We wait in hope for the LORD; *he is our help and our shield.*

—PSALM 33:20 CSB

I hate asking for help. As the firstborn of four girls, I've always been highly responsible and self-sufficient. I love helping others, but when I'm drowning, my first instinct is to do all I can to figure it out—*not* ask for a shoulder to lean on!

When I graduated high school, I was faced with so much newness that I knew nothing about. New responsibilities, new bills, new friendships . . . you get it. For the first time, I felt like I couldn't just "figure it out." I developed painfully high anxiety and was exhausted from the mental load of it all. There was so much I didn't know how to do. I *had* to ask for help, but I didn't realize asking for help was a gift. Having a community you can be honest with and who can help you is a privilege. God knew we would need help, so He gave us people.

Each one of us will have a moment where we come to the end of ourselves and our capabilities and realize we weren't made to do life on our own. We weren't built to carry the weight of the world or to suffer by ourselves. Only God can do that.

God is our help. He doesn't roll His eyes and groan while begrudgingly helping us get out of our mess. He delights in helping us. This is why Jesus sent the Holy Spirit. God is all-knowing, all-powerful, and fully capable of helping us through anything.

In Exodus 4:12, God helped Moses and gave him the words to say to the Israelites and to the ruler of Egypt. God told Moses, "Now go; I will *help* you speak and will teach you what to say." God helped and delivered the entire nation of Israel. His promise to help them is found throughout the book of Isaiah. In Isaiah 41:13, God told Israel, "For I am the LORD your God who takes hold of your right hand and says to you, Do not fear; I will *help* you." In the book of Daniel, God helped three Jewish men named Shadrach, Meshach, and Abednego. He saved them from being burned alive in a fiery furnace!

And guess what? The God of the Bible is the same God we have today.

If you're feeling weighed down and there's something you need, your Help is already here. Stop giving all your energy to worrying and wrestling through life on your own. God wants you to recognize your need for Him. (We need Him regardless of whether we think we do or not.) You are not a burden, and you weren't created to do everything—or anything—on your own. Next time you're in trouble or can feel yourself starting to drown, look to God. He delights in helping you. And like the Holy Spirit delights in helping us, we can delight in asking Him for help too.

FURTHER READING: PSALM 28:7

- *How often do you ask for help?*
- *Do you believe God wants to help? Why?*
- *Where in your life do you need God's help?*

BECAUSE GOD IS MY HELPER, I CAN TRUST THAT HIS WAY IS WISE AND RIGHT.

GOD IS COMPASSIONATE

When he saw the crowds, he had compassion on them, because they were harassed and helpless, like sheep without a shepherd.

—MATTHEW 9:36

Do you find it easy to believe that God cares about your soul?

We tend to think God cares about our performance. We work hard and try to do the right things. Meanwhile, God is rarely interested in our abilities—He's concerned about the posture of our hearts.

In Matthew 9, we get a close look at Jesus during His time on earth. Jesus forgave and healed a paralytic, called a tax collector to be His disciple, raised a girl from the dead, healed a sick woman, gave sight to two blind men, and freed one man from demons. What were Jesus's motives? Was He just showing off to the Pharisees who were against Him? Was He puffing Himself up to display His power as God?

No. Matthew 9:36 tells us Jesus looked at all the people in need, and He was *moved to compassion*. His motives were rooted in the fact that He loved the people and was deeply concerned about their souls.

Jesus's motive is still compassion—because God is compassionate. Jesus is deeply concerned about our well-being. When He sees us hurting, He is moved to empathy because He understands our pain.

We are all like lost sheep without a shepherd. We are broken and bruised by the world's onslaught of problems, in need of a Savior who will meet us in the mess. God doesn't wish we would handle the mess better. He's not interested in our ability to get ourselves out of it. He's not waiting to see if He'll *have* to save us. No.

Being deeply acquainted with suffering and pain, when God looks at us, He is moved to compassion. He understands our intricately woven stories of hardship and sorrow. He sees our grief. He knows our fear. Satan wants us to believe that God is far-off. He wants us to believe that God can't be wrapped up in our lives because He is too good to interact with us.

But God is deeply concerned about *you*. He sees your suffering, worry, and effort. He is with you. Like the friend you've always wanted or the parent you've always desired, God looks at you with compassion and holds you tightly as He calls you deeper into His presence.

Fall into His warm embrace. Let Him help you. His compassion is genuine, and His motive is love.

Further Reading: Isaiah 49:10

- *Do you believe that God has compassion toward you? If that's hard for you to believe, why?*
- *How have you seen God's compassion in your own life?*
- *How can God's compassion impact the way you live?*

BECAUSE GOD IS COMPASSIONATE, I CAN TRUST THAT HE UNDERSTANDS ME.

NONE LIKE HIM

WRITE

INFINITE

DOODLE

OMNIPOTENT

WRITE

ALL-KNOWING

WRITE

DOODLE

EVERYWHERE

WRITE

DOODLE

GOOD

WRITE

DOODLE

PROMISE KEEPER

WRITE

DOODLE

SAFE PLACE

WRITE

DOODLE

LOVE

WRITE

DOODLE

SHEPHERD

WRITE

DOODLE

photo by Kariss Farris

ABOUT THE AUTHOR

ALENA FRANKLIN is an author, actress, and vocalist with a passion for sharing the hope of Jesus. She made her film debut in the Kendrick Brothers' *War Room* (2015) and returned to the screen in *The Forge* (2024). As a writer, she co-authored the *Lena in the Spotlight* series with her mother, Wynter Pitts, the founder of *For Girls Like You* Magazine.

Alena's journey has been shaped by both incredible success and deep loss. After her mother's passing in 2018, Alena's faith became her anchor, fueling her desire to encourage and equip girls and women to walk confidently in their identity in Christ. Through speaking, writing, and music, she continues to use her voice to inspire the next generation. She serves as a spokesperson for *For Girls Like You Ministries*. She and her husband, Caziah Franklin, reside in Nashville, Tennessee.